Toward the Theory of
Administrative Tethering

Toward the Theory of Administrative Tethering

Re-thinking Child Welfare Training amid Rationally Bounded Administrative Decision-Making and Collaborative Governance Processes

Kevin Marino and Robert James Wright

LEXINGTON BOOKS

Lanham • Boulder • New York • London

Published by Lexington Books
An imprint of The Rowman & Littlefield Publishing Group, Inc.
4501 Forbes Boulevard, Suite 200, Lanham, Maryland 20706
www.rowman.com

86-90 Paul Street, London EC2A 4NE

British Library Cataloguing in Publication Information Available

Library of Congress Cataloging-in-Publication Data

Names: Marino, Kevin, 1976- author. | Wright, Robert James, 1967- author.
Title: Toward the theory of administrative tethering : re-thinking child welfare training
    amid rationally bounded administrative decision-making and collaborative governance
    processes / Kevin Marino and Robert James Wright.
Description: Lanham : Lexington Books, [2022] | Includes bibliographical references. |
    Summary: "Toward a Theory of Administrative Tethering is the culmination of a
    seven-year commitment to investigate and explore the nature of collaboration,
    specifically in child protective services (CPS)"— Provided by publisher.
Identifiers: LCCN 2021051715 (print) | LCCN 2021051716 (ebook) |
    ISBN 9781793642943 (cloth) | ISBN 9781793642950 (ebook)
Subjects: LCSH: Child welfare—North Carolina—Case studies. | Social work
    administration—North Carolina—Case studies. | Interagency coordination—North
    Carolina—Case studies. | Public administration—Decision making—Case studies.
Classification: LCC HV742.N8 M37 2022 (print) | LCC HV742.N8 (ebook) |
    DDC 362.709756—dc23/eng/20211202
LC record available at https://lccn.loc.gov/2021051715
LC ebook record available at https://lccn.loc.gov/2021051716

Contents

Acknowledgments

This book could not be possible without the support of so many people Robert and I have around us. Of course, our families, and I must thank my beautiful bride Ashley for the many years of late nights and early mornings Robert and I have spent in conversation and writing. She was ever so patient and understanding. We thank God for the wisdom and pathways that lead us to the right people at the right time. I honestly would have never in a million years pictured being an author. So, Robert, I really must thank you for recognizing my potential and pushing us to the goal line. We have become brothers through this process.

As the brother I never had, Kevin I thank you for leadership and remaining steadfast to our mission and vision as documented in my calls that have spanned eight years. You are the very best. Likewise, to my parents, my three sisters—Ramona, Rebecca, and Rachel—and to my other brother, Ignacio, I owe you everything. And to Mary, you made this work!

Thank you to our amazing editors at Lexington Publishing for believing in our work. Joe and Carter, you two are so gracious to work with. Robert and I appreciate all the careful guidance and assistance through the review and editing process. The book art is more than we could have imagined. You two were in the right place at the right time for us and we look forward to making you proud you chose us and to the next work.

We also acknowledge the following individuals as they helped in ways that pushed Kevin and me closer to a goal line that at a certain point was hidden in a rather thick layer of fog.

Jacqueline Shiner, MPA, provided critical insights that served as the initial conceptual construct and foundation to the notion of tethering and helped to craft the Shiner-Wright model of collaboration. Thanks, Jacqueline.

Dr. Timothy Scheid provided keen insights concerning the realm of critical thinking and its application in the CPS realm. Tim's thoughts offered structure to realistic ways in which Administrative Tethering (AT) could be more effectively applied therein as reflected in chapter 5. Tim provided meaningful perspectives from the field of practice and helped Kevin and me to advance the notion of AT in this realm. Dr. Jennifer Hamburger, you are so humble and wise. Robert and I were always impressed with where your thoughts would take us in the realm of deep trust. Calculating such a flexible variable created many challenges along the way. Your persistence in working with us in AT is an incredible benefit to other leaders in public administration.

Dr. Angela Pitman-Vanderweide is a tenacious leader, visionary, and change agent. It has been a joy to watch you motivate and innovate well before it was a fad! Robert and I are thankful for the contributions you provided for the brain science found in reasoning and leadership skills. We know our audience will walk away equipped with fresh skills that work in public administration. The blend with our AT theory and skills was a complimentary match. Dr. Tanya Westbrook, you are a true friend. Robert and I were always impressed with your expert knowledge and energy as you engaged the topics of child welfare (CW) and social work. You continue to enhance the field and practice of CW in many ways. Thank you.

Dr. William Dwenger provided thoughtful reviews of the early stages of this work in terms of its consideration of today's complex bureaucratic setting. Likewise, Dr. Carol Matthews presented insights both as a practitioner and an academic involving collaboration in the public and nonprofit sectors. Dr. Sami Aldejwi was a source of sage advice concerning the analysis and evaluation of some of the more nuanced managerial dimensions of this topical area. As Sami and I both call the University of LaVerne our doctoral home, I was familiar with his conceptual "gems" of thought that he produced to advance our work during its mid-developmental phase.

John Huggins, ABD, proffered thoughtful additives to the literature review; he was able to identify highly relevant conceptual areas of collaboration as drawn from his careful attention to the details surrounding AT. Also, a big thank you goes to my former student, retired Marine, and now doctoral candidate Kenneth Powers, MPA, MA. Ken was able to integrate the conceptual areas of AT with the practitioner realm; this application offered further analytical findings surrounding the utility of AT. Nadeem O'duu furnished a meaningful review of those empirical methods and techniques that aligned with the mediation model of AT from an applied perspective. These insights helped Kevin and me to develop useful analytical and conceptual pathways pertaining to salient dimensions of our work. Finally, Dr. Jeffrey Ziomek provided early, ongoing help constructing key expressions of AT during our

Saturday call. I enjoyed these calls as he reminded me how warm it was in Florida and I retorted with the frigid temperatures in Salem, Massachusetts.

For the individuals noted here, Kevin and I say a collective thank you offer a heartfelt bravo!

Kevin and Robert

Introduction

I started in child protection services (CPS) 15 years ago. In the first week, I received a full case load and filed an emergency order to remove children from their home and place them in foster care. In the first six months, I experienced my first child fatality. In the third year, I uncovered an inter-generational familial sex trafficking case, which led to threats on my life and my family was being stalked. What in the blazes had I gotten myself and my family into? What was I exposing my family and children to? I thought all my years in behavioral health, substance abuse treatment and forensics prepared me to "help families and children stay together." No one truly prepared me for the darkest parts of CPS. Not even the state's training prepared me for the emotional, physical, and spiritual warfare that I accepted into my life. Some of you are probably thinking at this point, "just walk away!"

In my fourth year, I experienced two more child fatalities. One was a case I shared with two other child protection professionals at my home agency. The second case involved a baby exposed to thousands of rat bites. The second case belonged to a close colleague who worked in an agency near mine. Did you know many child protective professionals will work an entire career and not experience the darker side of the service? It is similar in the law enforcement profession who never experience having a gun drawn on them and they have never drawn their gun on a suspect. Are you comparing child protection with law enforcement? Absolutely! The nature of the decisions both professionals engage in daily result in life or death. I am completely uncertain at this point if enough people understand the true dangers of working in CPS. The emotional and psychological distress also known as vicarious trauma and secondary stress has been researched and shown to be a reality. I just do not believe enough people, or the right people, have looked hard enough at what can change the systemic cycle of psychological and emotional degradation in this profession.

It is tragic to hear or experience the loss of a child. It deepens the wound when the cause of death is believed to be preventable from a logical and reasonable position. The statement, "this child's death was preventable," elicits actions to exact justice from the responsible persons. Justice born from the atrocity of a child's death is unquenchable, and so it seeks not only the immediate perpetrator but also anyone with knowledge that potentially, if they intervened, or performed a better service, could prevent such. The impaling traumatic response leaves an omnidirectional wake behind it. One is the family and friends of the victim, and the second is the child protection worker, and their organization, who trusted to keep the child safe. Justice, grief, and sympathy are afforded to the child's family and community; however, the child protection workers are most often left bankrupt and destitute and succumb to the blunt force trauma of a lonely guilt. More times than not, these child protection staff are abandoned by their organizations and the overall system because it is easier to sacrifice one lamb to protect the heard, which also needs correction.

I am not defending all child protection workers and their organizations. It is incredibly important we, as a community, sift the insidious from the ignorance on the winnowing fork as not to burn the wheat with the chaff in the insatiable fire of justice. My hope is that the audience of this book are from child protection professions, and this elicits examples from your experience. Even if you have not lived through or known someone close to you that has lived through, or they are going through it right this very moment, you hear or read the news stories of children passing at the hands of abuse or neglect. In case you are just starting your career or reading this from another discipline read the case examples below so that we can discern the insidious from the ignorance.

Zahra Baker went missing October 9, 2010, in Hickory, North Carolina (NC). CPS received reports and provided investigative services in July and August of 2010. According to what is reported in the media, CPS did not find evidence this child was abused or neglected. Zahra's autopsy indicated she died from "homicidal violence." Is it a case that the parents were able to keep the abuse and neglect hidden from CPS? Where clues or indicators present the CPS professionals could have recognized with more time or better training? When no harm or sign of abuse or neglect is apparent was there signs of impending danger or risk? The stepmother is currently serving a 20-year sentence for second-degree murder, and Zahra's father moved back to Australia.

August 16, 2021, a three-year-old in Mobile AL died from "abuse over time" at the hands of the child's mother and the mother's boyfriend. This breaking news is too new at the time of writing this book. The child's death from "abuse over time" is a salient reason to include it as an example of injustice. We do not know if CPS was involved or if anyone had reported allegations of maltreatment of this child. Abuse of this nature can go completely undetected until it is too late. How? Children can suffer injuries from abuse or neglect, and are never taken to the doctor, or they go and the injuries still go undiagnosed. An injury can be diagnosed, and a reasonable explanation is given from a parent or caretaker. Prior injuries could heal and go undetected even if the child is taken to the doctor. There is no certain method that can be applied to detect all malfeasant behavior.

An 11-year-old boy found by law enforcement handcuffed to a porch with a dead chicken hanging from his neck in November of 2013. It was a form of punishment for not following directions. A child protection supervisor was licensed to foster children in NC County. This person's position was used as leverage to foster children to abuse them. This story exposes the more insidious side of maltreatment of children. Other stories of child welfare (CW) professionals falsifying documents and even having sexual relations with children by those charged with protecting them presently exists in the system. How then, when parents and caretakers fail to do so, are communities to find any hope to keep children safe?

The weight and nature of the work CW professionals are tasked with executing carry life and death consequences. So heavy it then seems reasonable that each of these professionals receives the best education and training to prepare them to skillfully, thoughtfully, and empathically provide interventions that prevent and protect children from further harm or danger. The cases mentioned in these examples create an omnidirectional wave of distrust for the child protection system. The lack of trust results in less reports of abuse and neglect, less cooperation from community partners, increases in micromanaging casework and outcomes, and repeat maltreatment.

As a mid-level public manager, I ask myself, "What has really changed?" Are less children going into the foster care system? Is there a decrease in repeat maltreatment of children? Has the retention of CW professionals improved? If I am truly honest, even though our system has seen many changes in law, policy, funding, and practices, I conclude that not a lot has changed. Some may even argue it is worse with the onset of the opioid epidemic, human trafficking, and reviewing racial disparities. I needed to find a way as a mid-level manager to change my home organization and have broader impacts at the state and federal levels. I was tired of leaders and managers making decisions that were too far removed from the work, and frankly never done the work. When I met Bob, he listened to my story and struggle, we found hope in the theory and emerging practice in what we term as "Administrative Tethering" (AT).

Toward a Theory of Administrative Tethering is the culmination of a seven-year commitment to investigate and explore the highly complex and chaotic nature of collaboration, specifically in CPS. This journey began with an atypical relationship between a doctoral student practicing in CPS and an academic mentor. Research conducted to investigate challenges in the decision-making process between frontline workers and supervisors leads to grand-scale questions about the holistic system of CPS and why it appears to be in a state of inertia. Examination of the totality of the CPS system in NC necessitated more in-depth study into effective interventions proven to foster change relevant to improve service delivery for frontline staff and to engage executive leadership at the local and state levels. The mission of CPS is to ensure the safety of children by mediating danger and threat. All CPS actors must function in a highly coordinated fashion to provide the orderly delivery of this social product to the public as needed and as expected.

The complex systems containing thousands of actors tend to overcomplicate solutions in various ways. The competing imperatives throughout the system amplify the distracting background noise by introducing short-term solutions that, in the end, consume valuable resources without producing social change. Organizations at the local, state, and federal level, which make up the institution CW (or CPS) are vulnerable to organizational sicknesses such as secondary stress, toxic culture, high turnover, lack of interest in joining the profession, and a host of other ailments. As such, the issue is one of institutional health and fitness.

At the center of these complex social organizations are the people. The services and products are rendered to produce a change in human behavior. Attempts to procure tools such as an evidence-based practice model, a new assessment rubric, or new computer software cannot circumvent the human aspect existing at the core of the decision matrix. Today's advanced technology and inundation of information confound the core organizational processes by limiting human potential in the name of efficiency. Such perplexing behaviors can only be tempered by the strong transforming leader who thrives in an organization that values innovation and adaptation. Years of in-depth study in the field of public administration, collaboration, and decision-making intersected with the genius of Professor Herbert A. Simon's scholarship. This intersection rekindled and cultivated a fresh perspective culminating in AT. This notion has emerged as highly valuable to implementing those needed high-quality improvements to enhance the delivery of those critical protective services designed to prevent and address instances of child endangerment in NC.

In this book, we contend that collaboration is a proverb, as Simon infers in his discourse pertaining to this notion as it manifests in the conduct of public administration. The subject is relevant to the management of complex organizational structures. Simon instructs the classical administration principles (the proverbs) are "mutually contradictive," and are subject to proper scientific analysis to best understand how to apply them given the organizational setting (Simon, 1947 p. 50). We engage such analysis to assess our hypothesis.

The chapters outlined in this book introduce and advance the conceptual areas of collaboration theory. Simon's work is stitched into each chapter, and his perspectives provide the binding agent to the emerging AT framework. AT can be conceptualized as a strategic management design that employs a series of interagency bonding actions and techniques to address the multidimensional nature of a complex, pressing public problem. The AT manager binds collaborative partners together via transcending, multi-messaging modalities; this intervention aims to instill high levels of trust, value, accountability, and motivation at the partnering level. Simon prescribes that although this coordination is warranted, it must carefully balance its costs against its returns (2002, 2000, 1962). The implications regarding the utility and relevance of AT will be examined in terms of Simon's important perspective regarding coordination. This cognitive foray will be attended throughout the book's chapters. This work concludes with the identification of new research and its potential utility and overall impact for both the practitioner and academic.

Chapter 1 introduces the initial creation of tethering based on Robert Wright's work surrounding the workforce investment act's complexities on the eastern seaboard. It travels through the seminal and relevant research pertaining to collaboration revealing vulnerable areas requiring further study. It then provides AT's evolution via the Shiner-Wright Model (SWM) of tethering as applied to e-procurement contracts in federal spaces. It concludes with an anchoring to Simon's bounded rationality (BR) and ND notions and introduces AT's operational aspects.

Chapter 2 describes a conditional example in which AT is crafted in the complex area of NC's CW system. The first practice in AT is to examine the institutional ecology outlining those salient historical events that have confounded the NC's CW system, and the actors operating inside. Such a condition identified by the AT manager rallies through missional motivation. Missional motivation lodged in trust, value, and accountability fashions a tethered ecology. In this example involving ten home CPS agencies in the western region of NC the AT manager's second practice is to focus on relationship and the mission versus transactions. It is within this ecology that the relationship life cycle transpired and rendered a set of high-quality relationships. The high-quality relationships diffused a power equilibrium within which the Western-10 Collaborative has flourished. This collaborative, moreover, provides a layer of protection that insulates the AT work from the troubles associated with the complex micro and macro systems encountered as its mission is advanced.

Chapter 3 demonstrates the AT framework's application as aligned with Simon's notions of BR and near decomposability (ND). The idea of BR is celebrated in scholarship from various disciplines. We observe the combination of BR with ND as fuel for AT theory. BR and ND aid in calibrating the application of the AT intervention. AT propositions function as an additional resource to successfully guide the AT manager's movements through the bureau's malaise. The AT intervention counters the negative impacts of local and state systems entrenched in inertia. Our quantitative analysis provides initial evidence demonstrating AT's effectiveness and a requirement to focus on trust as relationships are formed in the tethered ecology.

Chapter 4 considers emerging research signifying an imperative to attain a deep level of trust among actors to accomplish its mission. The AT intervention can influence an organization's development trajectory and thus expand the scope of its membership to reinforce the formation of a nucleus of trust that is highly effective. Great care and evaluation are necessary to allocate time and resources to ensure our readers leave the pages behind with a strong understanding of the AT framework's lynchpin. The case for trust is demonstrated through three research projects conducted at various points in time. This overall exploration and investigation use quantitative and qualitative methods to extrapolate findings from the systems levels. The results manifest two potential pathways requiring the AT manager's attention. The first is successful tethering produces trust germane to keeping the organizational members focused on the mission. The second organization, untethered and not attentive to trust, is rendered unfit and will experience great difficulty adapting. Lastly, the value of the organizational members corporately and individually correlates with the strength of trust.

Chapter 5 deconstructs the three process treatments from the AT framework, which the AT manager relies upon to attend to trust, value, accountability, and motivation. Collaboration networks are fashioned and maintained with interagency members. The premise of relationship is the prerequisite for crafting a tethered ecology. We argue collaboration must be established in high-quality relationships cultivated in trust and value. Forming relationships of this nature takes time and attention to various details and a genuine authenticity to be in a relationship with a potential member. AT applies the family life cycle (FLC) as a guide to establishing such relationships and provides the manager with treatment methods designed to recognize and address BR of self and others. The attributes of trust and value play an integral part in this process. As relationships mature, feedback mechanisms engage in a set of exchanges between dyads that cascade into the larger groupings. The intentional feedback is a commitment and application of messaging among members. It promotes ND by addressing BR, which instills trust and value in the fit organization's name.

The second and third processes are interrelated but require some individual attention. AT considers the applications of neuro-leadership. The four essential characteristics of trust, value, accountability, and motivation, as summarized in the AT framework, are further deconstructed into the eight neuro-leadership traits. Breaking the process down in this fashion identifies specific treatment areas the AT manager must attend to high-quality relationship-building. Lastly, the multitude of encircling decisions engaged by the AT manager and the tethered ecology reveals the critical thinking skillset's vital application. Engagement in a complex ecological system by the AT manager compels strategic actions based upon a critical thinking capacity that functions at a higher level as exercised in an omnidirectional fashion.

Moreover, the AT manager also has a responsibility to inculcate the tethered community in a push-and-pull system to produce agile and formidable decisions to advance the mission. To adequately address the critical thinking realm, we gathered relevant material specific to this thinking mode and applied it to the child protection service function, and then tailored a three-lens process to comport with its decision-making infrastructure. This approach considers those quantitative characteristics that can be studied via administrative data and tracing strategy to collect indicators of BR and foster ND manifestations.

Chapter 6 concludes the incredible insights captured in the application of Simon's scholarship in a collaborative framework. AT taught us an important lesson regarding the practice-theory interchange. Simon's wisdom lent us welcomed prescriptions here. He has repeatedly cautioned that scholarly attention must remain steadfast in its effort for theory to be construed as relevant to the practice. The "how to" of such a task does not come easy—it calls for a steady flow of critical thinking. We then focused our attention on how public administration theories can circulate within a milieu that is familiar to a cadre of practitioners. For us, Simon's prescription regarding the utility of theory was taken to heart. Out of necessity, we maintained a steady presence at the AT helm for the CPS practice to value public administration diagnostics' utility on a lasting basis.

This work seeks to make meaningful use of the body of knowledge provided by Herbert Simon; Simon's intellectual legacy can best be characterized as herculean in terms of the knowledge edifice that it has built and ocean-like in terms of its scope of influence. In the end, it is anticipated that this work will provide its singular grain of knowledge in the attempt to contribute to such an intellectual domain as interpreted here.

Chapter 1

Toward a Theoretical Construct of Administrative Tethering

Examination of H. Simon's seminal work, *Administrative Behavior* (1948), relates to and informs vital dimensions of the work undertaken in collaboration with his perspective of the "proverbs" of public administration. Simon instructs that applying the "principles" of public administration (efficiency, unity of command, a span of control, etc.) should be construed as proverbs. They are characterized as proverbs in that they are more appropriately seen as criteria for describing and diagnosing administrative situations (Simon, 1997, p. 42).

The notion of the proverb can relate to collaboration in that those individuals who develop the innovative solutions for today's collaboration may not necessarily share the sense of urgency typically associated with those cost-control directives from upper management. This condition can become problematic to the collaboration when its innovators instinctively draw upon their expertise to justify their remedies while seemingly ignoring the cost-control imperatives as carefully prescribed by its upper management. These interactions can dampen the enthusiasm and overall support for the collaboration at the stakeholder and operator levels.

Construing collaboration as a proverb of public administration encourages analysis centering upon crucial aspects of public programming. This analytical frame fosters a proper venue to augment existing cognition surrounding the conduct of public administration. Knowledge can accrue when considering how collaboration manifests at the granular level of public programming. This focus draws analytical attention involving the impact of the numerous interorganizational decisions and strategic actions upon the (effective) delivery of program services provided to the public. Indeed, this book's central theme is to understand better how a set of ten counties were able to work together over seven years to realize some dramatic improvements surrounding the delivery of child

1

protection services (CPS) within their respective jurisdictions. When construed as a PA proverb, understanding grew as to the complex set of interactions central to the decision-making processes of this collaboration. In this collaboration, exemplar areas of authority and expertise helped frame those vital decisions related to its sustained success. This overall finding reinforces the claim that collaboration aligns with Simon's construct of the public administration proverb.

The rules that govern and frame those expert-driven, decision-making dealings, intrinsic to the above collaboration, should be interpreted as malleable and situational-driven such that contradictory (administrative and tactical) action should be understood as equally valid from the analytical vantage. Both (contradictory) approaches could be applied in equal measure to effectively manage the complex decision-making modalities intrinsic to the realm of collaboration (Simon, 1997). These findings further suggest that today's public managers should focus on how their organization's hierarchical relationships can drive key actions of collaboration. The imperative to assemble *like-minded* actors for the meaningful collaboration impact may need to be deemed a secondary, if not tertiary, proposition.

Like-mindedness does not promote equilibrium, efficiency, unity of command, or span of control. Attempting to bind collaboration through like-mindedness is insufficient and allows supple opportunity to drift from the groups' purpose. One example, which will be discussed more in chapter 5 is the case of Rylan Ott in North Carolina (NC). His death came in the wake of NC's child welfare (CW) institution's poor performance as indicated by the Child and Family Services Review, which is the monitoring mechanism of the Administration of Children and Families at the federal level. A collaboration of academics, legislators, county commissioners, county managers, local CW leaders, and state officers came together to make sweeping changes. This group began its work in 2017 and was tasked with evaluating moving from a county- to a state-administered system, training, practice, and fiscal operations of CW (UNC – SOG, 2021). As of the writing of this manuscript in 2021 nothing has changed except a new law providing the state CW officers the ability to enforce sanctions against a local CW agency for poor performance. All of these like-minded stakeholders are passionate and well-intended, but in four years the CW institution nor the local organization receives any tangible changes to improve such a critical service. The North Carolina collaborative group was not tethered by the four tethering strands, which propel a group or organization in a specific direction over a period of time as noted by Simon, nor was the collaborative united by a singular mission. The group was inundated with information promoting a poverty of attention. AT offers middle managers proximal to the root issues the ability to create solutions and pathways via tethering to facilitate change through application of Simon's notions of bounded rationality (BR) and near decomposability (ND).

LITERATURE REVIEW

The public administration literature that has helped to build and shape the overall development of collaboration, as framed by the extant and future needs of both the academic and practitioner realms, can be distilled down to the following: first, the *sans hierarchy* perspective as exemplified and manifested in those collaborations that involve liked-minded experts and stakeholders; and second, those collaborations that are driven by a hierarchical structure that invokes a highly acute command-and-control posture. Importantly, however, a central, vital question is not explicitly raised by these two theory development areas. They leave unanswered as to *what* theoretical approach should be applied based upon the situational context encountered. To adequately address this fundamental query, an exhaustive assessment is needed. This review will contribute to the overall understanding of how evaluation criteria manifest as measures of collaboration effectiveness. The importance of this focus should not be underestimated. Implications are highly relevant from multiple vantages surrounding the effectiveness of collaboration and its eventual sustainability. The literature in this chapter highlights this notion as it explores some of the numerous, vexing challenges and opportunities intrinsic to the collaboration development and sustainability processes.

Theory Area—Collaboration: Local Precursors to Collaboration Participation

The literature surrounding collaboration demonstrates the importance of a set of new ideas and/or shared norms around which participants coalesce to form a collaborative. Literature also concerns the private sector involvement in collaboration (Younsung and Darnall, 2015; Delfini, 2014; Weber, 2009). This research has attended to those determinants of collaboration engagement. Findings have been proffered that the business entity tends to engage in collaboration when its interests align with the social problem that needs to be remedied (Younsung and Darnall, 2015; Delfini, 2014; Weber, 2009). These firms, in turn, can deem that their internal efforts cannot remedy this societal concern, and thus participate in joint problem-solving efforts with different social actors and stakeholders involved in the collaboration (Younsung and Darnall, 2014; Delfini, 2014).

Government and private sector engage in collaboration through those contractual arrangements in which the private entity provides a service to the government. The private sector entity may be part of a public project but has no interest in the project outside the private company's contractual work. Due to the cost associated with governance, it may become necessary to combine public and private sector resources to support the implementation of large infrastructure projects (Zakharina et al., 2020). This partnering arrangement is referred to as a public-private partnership (PPP) and provides the private sector entity a vested interest in the project. Why then might a private entity become involved with PPPs given their potential, for instance, to generate unforeseen project costs and general cost overruns? This type of collaboration aims to leverage long-term contract flexibility wherein innovative cost-sharing implementation approaches are designed to realize infrastructure projects that otherwise would not have materialized (Valila, 2020).

The private sector actors seek to participate and collaborate with social actors. Corporate social responsibility (CSR) highlights that such actors aim to bolster public trust and maintain an overall positive public perception (Kim, 2017, 2019). When a private company conducts business that is perceived for the social good, they are more likely to reduce their employee turnover, attract better-qualified employees, and increase positive consumer connection (Wang et al., 2019). One example of this is Microsoft and other tech firms working with local nonprofits and other stakeholders to develop their future headquarters in a manner that reduces their carbon footprint. Many have pledged to go carbon-free and work with nonprofits to fund projects to offset their carbon footprint. Many other organizations have done the same such as MacDonald's who worked throughout its supply chain to make their meat fit into specific "healthy categories."

Theory Area: Understanding What Shapes a Polycentric Governance System

Other areas of the literature have highlighted the import of considering the notion of the *risk hypothesis*; this perspective sees that actors embedded in governance systems in which there is the widespread risk of defection tend to form bonding structures, whereas those in low-risk systems bridging networks tend to take shape (Berardo and Lubell, 2016). This area of the literature also posits that complex governance systems depend on contextual variables, such as the institutions' stability, as analyzed from the frame of collaboration engagement (Berardo and Lubell, 2016). Polycentric governance is a system involving multiple policy-makers from multiple organizations for purposes of policy development. This approach to governance seeks to more effectively apply and consider policy issues with numerous federal, state, and local agencies with jurisdiction and/or impacted stakeholders, and so on (Hyman and Kovacic, 2020). Polycentric governance offers helpful insights into managing the many actors who align with the highly complex policy realm (Gil, 2018). Thus, organizational leaders need to understand the importance of collaboration with other organizations and agencies.

Theory Area: Collaborative Advantage

Collaboration research posits that an interorganizational coordination arrangement tends to form when its parties discern that a mutually beneficial "collaborative advantage" can be realized. In essence, these organizations recognize that through collective action, they can strategically capture a set of needed benefits not possible through actions of a solo nature (Molinengo and Stasiak, 2020; Rainey et al., 2016; Potapchuk, 2016). For example, the notion of collaborative advantage manifests when groups of nonprofits self-organize to form one parent organization. This business arrangement aims to reduce the individual nonprofit's financial burden for core operational and/or administrative services.

Theory Area: Collaborative Governance Effectiveness

Research has also found that relationships matter as mediated in a collaborative governance framework. Relational leadership has been found to have a positive influence upon the nature of those outcomes associated with a collaborative undertaking (Siddiki, Kim, and William, 2017; O'Leary, 2016; Conner, 2015). Beliefs and trust have been found to positively impact collaborative governance outcomes (Siddiki, Kim, and William, 2017; O'Leary, 2016; Conner, 2015). Scholarship on collaborative governance identifies several structural and procedural factors that consistently influence governance outcomes (O'Leary, 2016, Conner, 2015). A promising next step for collaborative governance research is to explore how these factors interact. Focusing on two dimensions of social learning—relational and cognitive—as outcomes of collaboration could provide essential insights about diverse belief constructs' influence upon relational learning (Siddiki, Kim, and William, 2017. Also, research suggests that raw self-interest needs matter in terms of engaging, collaborative governance; a policy needs not just to invoke the right incentives but also present them in the correct sequence and manner (Siddiki, Kim, and William, 2017; O'Leary, 2016; Conner, 2015).

Theory Area: Interlocal Collaboration

Research suggests that political similarities matter concerning the nature of meaningful collaboration. This literature highlights that those confluence areas help foster a useful collaborative undertaking (Song et al., 2017; and Andrew et al, 2015). This research also examines how political similarities (homophily) stimulate interorganizational collaboration patterns in an emergency response situation (Song et al., 2017; and Andrew et al., 2015).Findings indicate that political solidarity, formulated by chief elected officials of municipalities and council members, can broaden the scope of interorganizational collaboration by mitigating institutional collective action problems at the local level (Song et al., 2017; and Andrew et al., 2015). Sungkyunkwan and Jung, 2017; Andrew, Kyujin and Arlikatti, 2015).

Local governments increasingly confront policy problems that span the boundaries of their political jurisdiction. Interlocal collaboration is construed when a region of local governments cojoin to mitigate a problem held in common (Gjertsen, 2014). Such collaboration can emerge for other purposes, such as the infrastructure project with regional impacts. For example, the District of Columbia collaborated with other jurisdictions on a regional basis to build the METRO mass transit system. Collaboration networks that foster face-to-face interactions tend to promote social capital; this condition can encourage agencies and local governments to unite under the auspices of ad hoc planning organization. Such an entity can enhance the effectiveness involving the conduct of relevant bargaining and negotiating activities.

Theory Area: Collaboration and Leadership Impact Areas

Literature insights submit that inspirational motivation, as inculcated by the transformational leader, fuels collaboration; this condition generates a sense of cohesiveness among followers through the communication of such a shared vision (Sun and Henderson, 2016; Waugh Jr. and Streib, 2006). Because collaboration should be grounded in its members' everyday pursuits, a shared vision makes it possible to reduce individual isolation and thus generate more opportunities for collaboration (Sun and Henderson, 2016; Waugh Jr. and Streib, 2006). Moreover, transformational leadership fosters sharing ideas and knowledge and encourages employees to offer different points of view (Sun and Henderson, 2016; Waugh Jr. and Streib, 2006; Bass, 1985). The literature further highlights that leadership fosters effective collaboration as secured in a compelling vision's transformational power, rather than from hierarchy, rank, or standard operating procedures (Sun and Henderson, 2016; Waugh Jr. and Streib, 2006; Bass, 1985).

Theory Area: Factors That Promote Effective Networks

Partnerships can foster collaboration effectiveness. As measured by frequency of contact, relationships' strength shows that a high contact level between communities and organizational partners tends to contribute to high-performing networks (Shrestha, 2017; Yi, 2017). Network structures matter. For instance, states with high average closeness and average clustering in their governance networks have been found to be positively disposed to collaboration (Shrestha, 2017; Yi, 2017). A collaborative network consists of different organizations with different belief systems and values that work together to achieve a common goal. It is important to understand that individuals, groups in networks, and social networks are modeled by various centrality measures, including degree centralization and network density (Krnc & Skrekovski 2020). Social networks can be considered your friends, coworkers, and others you know to form an individuals' network. However, the network contemplated here is more extensive than a personal network. It incorporates the intricacies of economic models, services, organizations, and others working together to provide services and goods (Shutters et al., 2018). This network asks one to look at these interpersonal connections as conduits through which information and other dynamics flow (Jarvie, 2018). Every individual and group has a network that intertwines with many others. A suitable exemplar relates to the research collaboration between institutions to augment the circulation and generalizability of research.

Theory Area: Collaboration Engagement

Trust is a key, positive factor in the decision to collaborate, as suggested by the literature. To engage in and sustain collaboration, long-standing adversaries must first reveal information that would likely remain strategically hidden under traditional notice-and-comment rulemaking procedures (Zhang and Feeney, 2017; Feiock, Dankook, and Park, 2012; Bryer, 2009). Trust impacts upon the decision to engage in promising, successful collaborative undertaking at the organizational and individual levels. Sharing information through a high trust level creates opportunities for participants to discover more numerous and innovative solutions to environmental problems that otherwise would be beyond their reach (Zhang and Feeney, 2017; Feiock, Dankook, and Park, 2012; Bryer, 2009).

Research has also found that administrator and citizen "role" perceptions can influence the quality of responsive behavior in collaborative activity (Zhang and Feeney, 2017; Bryer, 2009). For instance, the more administrators are interested in long-term relational commitments with citizens, the more responsive they will be to citizens in a collaborative process (Zhang and Feeney, 2017; Bryer, 2009). Also, high trust levels among administrators and citizens tend to bolster administrative response to those involved in the collaborative process. Finally, those administrators interested in citizens' experiential knowledge have also been found to be more responsive to citizens' collaborative uncertainties (Zhang and Feeney, 2017; Bryer, 2009). The literature also suggests that public managers must regularly engage and interact with stakeholders in the external environment to deliver meaningful policy outcomes (Zhang and Feeney, 2017; Bryer, 2009). Examining the motivations behind such behavior is a critical component of understanding management in the modern era. Some studies suggest that actors with similar interests are more likely to form collaborative partnerships. This research has implications for further research involving the theories of representation and the social construction of collaboration (Zhang and Feeney, 2017; Bryer, 2009).

SUMMARY AND IMPLICATIONS OF THE LITERATURE

Construing collaboration as public administration proverb prompts further review concerning the research that examines *only* a selection of the criteria intrinsic to a collaboration's effectiveness (Simon, 1948). Such an analytical focus can emerge as faulty, for example, in those instances when today's public administration practitioner is presented with a "collaboration toolbox" as furnished by the academic realm. As bestowed with this self-help kit, the practitioner may be directed to apply a tool that does not necessarily align with the problem under examination. Indeed, this situation can be further exacerbated when a mix of practitioners assemble to engage in a collaborative. The situation becomes acute as these actors share both success and failure experiences from prior application of the same toolkit for problem-solving purposes. Issues relating to credibility and trust can emerge as each of these practitioners, as collaboration actors, espouse the use of a tool that is perceived as faulty by their collaboration colleagues; these negative perceptions can quickly doom the collaboration as stakeholder morale becomes toxic.

In sum, the need to conduct sophisticated analysis surrounding collaboration centers upon the aim to generate useful knowledge for a diverse set of collaboration stakeholders. The imperative to acquire such understanding centers upon a promising research agenda that is exemplified with the following query: *Why is a collaboration initiated in some instances and not in others, and why does collaboration fail in some instances yet is sustained in others?*

THE SHINER-WRIGHT COLLABORATION MODEL

The capacities and skills required to operate and manage within a collaborative (public) environment differ from those needed to manage within a single organization. Today's public managers must be cognizant that the collaboration will call for the simultaneous application of their management skills that align with prescriptions of the manager's home organizations and considers the demands fostered by an operating context in which the notion of a hierarchy is nonexistent. Collaboration is a process that involves a diverse group of organizations and actors, including public and private entities. Such a multidimensional operating condition assumes varying perspectives and venues of engagement. The Shiner-Wright Collaborative Model (SWM) provides a useful conceptual framework salient to the collaboration process (Wright, R. and Shiner, 2017; Wright, 2009). This framework effectively depicts those imperatives that drive action on the part of its actors and stakeholders as per the following venues of engagement (see figure 1.1).

The Home Organization

The home organization, within the collaborative setting, can be construed as the entity that issues the set of tasks and performance expectations as driven by a superior-subordinate relationship as framed by an institutionally prescribed, hierarchical operating and rule arrangement. In addition, a return on investment (ROI) is maintained and articulated from the top-down (Wright, 2009). Thus, participants must grapple with the various demands of their overhead executives while they attempt to anticipate the challenges inherent in terms of developing and maintaining a collaborative undertaking from both the immediate and long-term vantage (Wright, 2009). Attention will turn to notions such as aligning the demands of their home organization with the reality of engaging in a collaborative undertaking in which resources may be scarce and individual dispositions may not emerge as

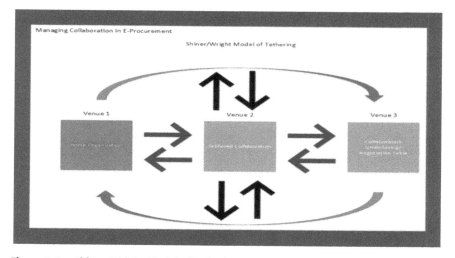

Figure 1.1   Shiner-Wright Model of Tethering. *Source:* Shiner and Wright (2017, p. 79).

necessarily cooperative in nature. This concern emerges as key when the initial planning actions revolve around the need to engage a specific collaborative approach. Pressures can manifest in diverse fashions as each participant defines their involvement in a dynamic development effort that involves multiple perspectives of command and control (Wright and Shiner, 2017; Wright, 2009).

Within the home organization (Venue 1), we see that each participant in the collaboration, whether public or private, comports to a set of performance expectations defined by those in command of the home organization (Wright and Shiner, 2017; Wright, 2009). In addition, a ROI conditions action by those managers tasked to the collaborative undertaking. Respective organizational imperatives can involve, for instance, challenges relating to "how" a ROI will materialize from their involvement in the overall collaborative undertaking (Wright and Shiner, 2017; Wright, 2009). The nature of the ROI can vary when multiple sectors are involved in the collaboration (Wright and Shiner, 2017; Wright, 2009). This difference can manifest in the requirements that govern the behaviors and actions of the manager tasked with oversight responsibilities related to the functioning of a particular collaborative undertaking (Wright and Shiner, 2017; Wright, 2009).

Tethered Operating Ecology

In the operating ecology of tethering (Venue 2), the public administrator attempts to mediate the home organization's demands while addressing the needs of the other collaboration participants (Wright and Shiner, 2017; Wright, 2009). While functioning in this tethered context, the manager must carefully assess the demands and needs of the home organization with those of the emerging collaboration (Wright, 2009). As the administrator tethers to the home organization, he/she must be mindful of those situations which may lead to job peril (Wright and Shiner, 2017; Wright, 2009).

Collaboration Arena

Within the collaboration arena (Venue 3), collaboration participants engage as framed with the reality that scarce organizational resources define the bounds of (collaborative) activities and action. This burden must be approached in a cautious, measured fashion (Wright and Shiner, 2017; Wright, 2009). The manager must continue to comport action with the prescribed mandates of the home organization as the nature of the complex problem is assessed and contemplated (Agranoff, 2003, 2004; Goldsmith et al., 2004; Meek et al., 2006, Campbell, 2012, Shakya, 2015).

SHINER-WRIGHT MODEL IMPLICATIONS

Venue 1 Implication Area. The (tethered) public manager, as a collaboration participant, must attend those opportunities to leverage a limited resource base (Wright and Shiner, 2017; Wright, 2009). This imperative will primarily draw upon the manager's strategic planning, negotiation, and interpersonal skills. The manager must craft an approach that strategically identifies areas of flexibility inherent in the construct of the ROI mandates of the home organization.

Venue 2 Implication Area. The tethered public manager must balance the budget pressures with those experts' solution development efforts ensconced in the collaboration as its core participants. For instance, careful mediation can enable the tethered manager to effectively proffer innovative solutions through the creation of (fiscally) efficient and effective partnering with industry (Wright and Shiner, 2017; Wright, 2009). Again, this creative development initiative must align with overall the ROI mantra that permeates the temporal nature of the collaborative undertaking

Venue 3 Implication Area. The tethered manager must exercise care when knowingly engaging in actions that directly bear upon the design scope of a highly innovative collaboration initiative. This care must be exercised given the promise of this initiative to allay the complex problem that serves as the *raison d'etre* for the collaborative. If the manager intervenes in a slipshod manner, then his credibility is likely to suffer irreparable damage as perceived by the operators, actors, and stakeholders of the collaboration (Wright and Shiner, 2017; Wright, 2009).

SHINER-WRIGHT MODEL IMPACT AREAS

Collaboration Inception. The early understanding as to the nature of the collaboration can foster a more effective management approach surrounding its coordination processes. Such effectiveness is rooted in the notion, for instance, that home organization alignment with the (new) management approach is secured (by the tethering manager) prior to engaging in the overall collaborative/coordination process.

Home organization leaders need to be informed early in the process of mission, goals, and tasks of the collaboration effort (Venues 1 and 2). An early endorsement from the home organization will assist with support from the home organization for changes to collaboration efforts and final approval of collaborative recommendations. The AT manager should build a clear understanding of the operational environment as well as any political ramifications associated with the participant's home organization requirements, mission, and objectives.

A clear understanding of the operating environment can help effectively assess and address the rise of potential objections to the collaborative undertaking before it is initiated and provides early warning of expectations for home organizations to plan for participation in the requested collaborative effort.

Home organizations are then empowered with the right information to provide the right personnel and support for collaboration prior to the first collaboration meeting. This area involves continuous assessment, monitoring, and evaluation of progress to adjust the purpose, direction, and motivation. Changes to gain needs to be made available to collaboration group members to ensure that home organizations are afforded the opportunity to adjust continued support (Wright and Shiner, 2017; Wright, 2009).

Stakeholder Disposition. Understanding the disposition of stakeholders allows for the effective application of AT management techniques to proactively design response strategies given the (dynamic) context in which the interagency effort operates. Such a stratagem can provide the group leader insight into potential concerns that may arise from specific members in the group. Early indications of the types and degree of situations that may occur allow the group leader to begin development or adjust AT Management Framework.

Disposition of the stakeholder within the collaborative effort dictates the level of understanding and application of the collaborative endeavor to the home organization (Venues 1, 2, and 3). A stakeholder's position and overall knowledge of the home organization is a determining factor in the level of input the stakeholder has to the collaborative effort (Wright and Shiner, 2017; Wright, 2009). The collaboration group leader in exercising AT leadership skills can adjust group management skills relevant to the dispositions of a member of the group. Understanding stakeholder dispositions need to occur early in the collaboration process to understand stakeholders' makeup before proceeding with detailed discussion and development of solutions to the issue under consideration (Wright and Shiner, 2017; Wright, 2009). The AT manager can apply multiple formal and informal communication pathways to address those issues as they arise.

Collaboration Diffusion. The diffusion of collaboration means that information flow between group members and home organizations will increase and be processed accordingly (Venues 2 and 3). Efforts on the part of the public manager providing oversight of the collaborative effort mean that coordination and flow of information will be key (Wright and Shiner, 2017; Wright, 2009). Changes and updates concerning the functional nature of the collaboration need to be managed to ensure that the information available represents the true nature of progress being made through collaborative efforts. It ensures that stakeholders, innovators, and home organizations remain current on any adjustments impacting the overall functional condition of the collaboration.

Collaboration Mobilization. The AT manager maintains a focus on intrinsic and external factors associated with a collaborative effort (Venues 1, 2, and 3). They serve to monitor any changes related to group membership and those adjustments due to daily turbulence intrinsic to the political, economic, social environment. This deep understanding can help the AT manager maintain the steady application of collaborative actions as manifested in a set of needed coordination processes (Wright and Shiner, 2017; Wright, 2009).

Tethering Initiated. The tethered manager attends to the continued assessment of the collaborative process and utilization of tethering techniques and skills. Upon initiation of Administrative Tethering (AT), continuous evaluation of the evolving situation is necessary to ensure that tethering activities are efficient and timely.

A continuous assessment of the collaborative process and utilization of tethering techniques necesstitates that the AT manager maintain a keen focus upon home organization leadership disposition, the nature of the (changing) requirements (i.e., administrative, budgetary, policy, etc.) intrinsic to the nature of collaborative undertaking, and those emerging concerns and/or dense problem areas as expressed by collaboration group members (Venues 1, 2, and 3). The assessment can manifest in an evaluation plan that can consist of internal reviews and external evaluations. Internal assessments provide an understanding of the collaboration group's effectiveness based on the day-to-day functions and activities of the collaboration group. External assessments provide home organizations an opportunity to review the value of their designated representative as a member of the collaboration group.

Assessment and evaluation results focus on the strengths and weaknesses of interaction and effectiveness of home organization representatives within the workings of the collaboration group and, most notably, how responsive collaboration group leaders are to home organization expectations. Collaboration group leaders require feedback from home organization senior leadership for continued support and participation in the collaborative effort.

Core Tethering Conducted. Core Tethering involves the conjunction of Venues 1, 2, and 3. The AT manager must attend to the (ongoing) scope of demands posed by the internal and external factors that necessitate a need for changes in the dynamics of the group, all communications between collaboration group leaders and home organization leadership, and results of any relevant (impact/performance) assessments and evaluations.

SUMMARY

Shiner and Wright (2017) demonstrate that such Collaboration Venues provide an area in which the various collaborative entities can effectively engage in a problem-identification and problem-resolution system. The nature of this operating ecology can and should be considered from the *tethering* framework as prescribed by the Shiner-Wright Collaboration Model; this framework furnishes useful insights and offers meaningful guidance from a management vantage (Wright and Shiner, 2017; Wright, 2009). Shiner and Wright (2017) highlight that:

> Collaboration transpires through a variety of communication channels while mediating complex, ever-changing operating ecologies that are driven by a diverse set of personalities. These ecologies can be influenced by 1) one's home organization; 2) the transitional space in which the participants of the collaboration must reconcile the often unrelenting oversight of their home organization while attempting to develop key (formal/informal) partnering arrangements within the emerging collaboration; and 3) the "area" in which the collaboration is developed, planned, and codified. The participants who ultimately are organizationally tasked with the responsibility to accrue benefits from a collaborative undertaken must quickly become experts managing developmental activities in these three venues. (p. 94)

This construct can help to foster an optimum problem-solving capacity for those highly skilled, mid-level public managers who, one morning, find themselves tasked to a newly formed collaboration whose sole purpose is to address an intimidating, historical public problem that has plagued their organization. This challenge is made further demanding for these managers as they now find themselves tethered between two imposing, collaboration operators. At the same time, they try to make sense of the fog-like ecology in which they must apply their refined, professional skills (Wright, 2009).

Managers who find themselves in this predicament must attempt to reconcile a set of demands as driven by highly complex challenges. These managers must contend with the overarching challenge to deliver effective solutions to their leadership in a timely manner. The manager will now need to coordinate a unique group of stakeholders with competing, complex interests, and dispositions as motivated by the ecological context of their home organization. Initially, this individual can consult the literature and find no shortage of tools that promise to help surmount those intractable design challenges that stymie the construct of an effective, interagency initiative. Mounting frustration will soon emerge as numerous tools are applied as prescribed without impact. Eventually, this frustration will transition to anger such that the collaboration will cease to exist.

Central to this conundrum is the organization. Simon informs us that organizations assume a pivotal role in today's conduct of human affairs due to their power to organize people to carry out highly complex activities from a service production perspective (Simon, 1962, 2000, 2002). This extraordinary power is rooted in the ability of the *effective* organization to motivate, inculcate a sense of identity, and foster loyalty among its individual members (Simon, 1962, 2000, 2002). Simon posits that this capacity is intrinsic to the notion that today an *organizational economy* frames, drives, and defines the nature of human affairs (Simon, 1962, 2000, 2002). Indeed, the organization is constantly subjected to a host of ecological, multifaceted forces that ultimately compel it to adapt and, in turn, evolve (or not).

The ability to evolve involves the extent to which the given organization strategically employs, and processes coordination techniques proportionate with the problem(s) that it must address. A measure of organizational fitness manifests in the benefits that the organization accrues by conducting these coordination activities while attempting to reconcile its burdensome costs. Simon provides that the fit organization holds down these costs by implementing highly efficient interagency initiatives through its subunit infrastructure. Simon terms this organizational property as nearly decomposable (Simon, 1962, 1996, 2002). Organizations convey the property of ND as related to its cachet of nearly decomposable federations of subsystems (Simon, 1996, 2002). This type of structural construct manifests in those ND arrangements designed to improve adaptability and reduce the fragility of the organization (Simon, 2002).

The notion of ND is an important conceptual foundation upon which a large set of scholarship has been developed since its introduction by Simon (1962, 2000, 2002). Importantly, the framework of ND provides a realistic set of determinants of the fit organization; this condition portends the longevity of an organization due to its capacity to efficiently and effectively mitigate those forces that can challenge its very existence (Simon, 1962, 2000, 2002). This knowledge carries further implications concerning the amorphous areas, such as the preservation of the social product that today's organizations help to provide in a democratic society.

ND applies to organizational activities that transpire within the organizational setting and that are subject to the control of a singular hierarchical reporting arrangement. Public managers, however, often must address complex problems that call for them to engage in "external" interorganizational actions and relations while navigating an ecology that is high in uncertainty and lacks a formal hierarchical arrangement from a command-and-control vantage. A central implication of this interagency operating arrangement is that the interorganizational undertaking lacks the property of ND. This deficiency prompts a review of the literature to identify a theoretical framework suitable for application purposes by the practitioner when contemplating an interagency undertaken requiring coordination/collaboration activities. Such a wanted theory, however, does not exist despite the many collaboration (*coordination*) "toolkits" as sourced from the practitioner and academic areas to a generation of seasoned managers (Simon, 1962, 2000, 2002).

Pathways to AT

Any theory designed to assist the public manager to fashion a suitable remedy approach to the public problem that begets an interagency response construct will be constrained by the need to provide for a costly (collaboration/coordination) processing infrastructure. The management challenges do not cease here. Design challenges can be agency-specific yet impact upon the operational efficiency of all coordination activities. Such a set of impacts threaten the ability of an organization and/or organizations to adapt to and, in turn, evolve given the dimensions of the complex problem that has (historically) plagued this organization (others) (Simon, 1962, 2000, 2002). This dilemma inevitably places this organization in an uncertain position; its leadership must reconcile the notion that their actions (or inactions) can embroil other organizations. Nonetheless, such an interagency entity remains subject to a coordination/collaboration process that can be deemed fickle and unwieldy at best (Simon, 1962, 2000, 2002). Such a scenario characterizes today's conduct of public administration when considering those complex public problems involving multiple public organizations at the various levels of government. A core question that materializes: *How, then, do today's public problems weaken the mitigation capacity of those interagency coordination initiatives despite their design by the exceptionally complex public, talent-rich organizations who base their actions in a culture of science?*

Simon provides critical insight and direction to those public administrators who lead, manage, and carry out intricate, interagency coordination tasks in response to a complex problem as encountered (1962, 2000, 2002). Simon's notions of the organizational economy and of ND contain important conceptual guidance that can ameliorate the lifetime challenges posed by these problems. Simon theorizes that these notions specifically manifest in the promise of the amalgamating capacity of the modern organization (1962, 2000, 2002). The leadership of today's modern organization strategically delegates management (oversight) responsibility pertaining to its core organizational initiatives. However, the profitable outcomes of such a decision can become confounded and sullied by the misguided actions of its organizational actors and/or operators. The behavior of such individuals becomes toxic as they act upon their self-interests rather than the priorities of the organization. If not adjusted, this condition can mature into a serious public problem that compels a concerned public to turn to those who govern to produce a response. An interagency collaborative may soon be ushered to the fore and construed as *the* panacea to address this public concern. From a more precarious vantage, the organization(s) may settle on an incomplete mitigation design. Such care-lessness can come at a steep price if the root cause(s) of the complex problem remains untreated.

This overarching design challenge prompts a holistic examination as to the nature of its operational dimensions (see Figure 1.2). A wise organizational leader may turn to the management ranks and designate one of the more seasoned managers to help to design a suitable remedy intervention under the umbrella of the overall interagency undertaking. This manager will be tethered to the home organization as he/she engages in coordination activities within the confines of the interagency development venue. The central aim of this interagency coordination approach is to fashion a realistic plan of action to mitigate the given problem. This interorganizational intervention will draw upon the manager's well-honed communication, interpersonal, and analytical skills as he/she functions administratively in a tethered context. The relevant implications of this context can be approximated through the conceptual lens of AT (Marino & Wright, 2019, 2020).

AT harnesses the important features of ND as it proffers a management intervention that imbues a sense of import and urgency among those actors who will carry out coordination activities of the interagency undertaking without a formal system of control (Simon, 1962, 2000, 2002). Moreover, this intervention seeks to temper any rush to action by the leaders of the impacted organizations. Such collective action may, nevertheless, hasten a solution that results in a set of faulty problems, mitigation prescriptions. This deficiency can promulgate a collaborative construct that is laden with complexity yet remains ineffective in nature. This condition is rooted in a decision-making fallacy that compels one to assume that the complexity of action will amend the complex nature of the problem as initially perceived. This fallacy fosters a paradox in that the inherent complexity of such an ill-equipped solution will help guide the tethering manager to effectively render AT expertise therein. The tethering manager, focusing all attention upon the careful design of the AT intervention, can more effectively locate and target the needed management and subject matter expertise to better understand the nature of the extant, complex problem. Importantly, such enhanced cognition will help to deliver an intervention that is highly effective from both impact and cost measures (Simon, 1962, 2000, 2002).

A meaningful AT intervention approach plan will apply suitable manage-ment resources as well as the appropriate subject matter expertise to arrive at a realistic, effective problem design. This knowledge promotes analytical precision as to the tools that must be marshaled to dampen the impact of the given problem, adjust its development trajectory, and provide the needed pro-tocols and assets to manage and control the originating conditions and forces intrinsic to its operating ecology. The AT intervention can then foster and

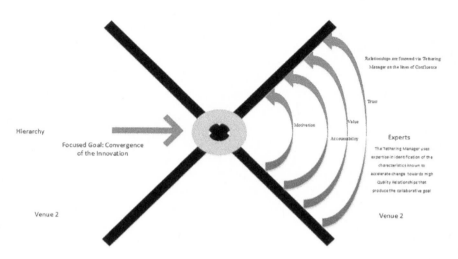

Figure 1.2   The Marino-Wright Administrative Tethering Model. *Source*: Figure created by authors.

align a management-driven research agenda to produce innovative, problem-remedy tools. The tethering manager catalyzes this outcome via the careful, measured coordination of highly complex research activities as they transpire between the academic and practitioner realms.

AT and the Evolution of the Complex Problem

From a practical vantage Simon (1962, 2000, 2002) notes that the organizational economy maintains two key provisions. First, it provides a balancing mechanism in terms of the diffusion of power within a democratic society, and second, it provides for the social product (Simon, 1962, 2000, 2002). The fit organization, rapidly responding to the burdens of evolution, will maintain its ability to deliver these public necessities in a fluid manner (Simon, 1962, 2000, 2002). Its ability to adapt in such an effective fashion will help this entity to deliver the social product as promised. This assurance is related to and dependent upon an operating ecology that sustains a diffusion of power through a check and balancing system as enabled by today's organizational economy (Simon, 1962, 2000, 2002). This notion can be examined and considered at both the macro and micro-levels. For this conceptual deliberation, the micro-level is the focus of interest. The public organization is not spirited to place the public in harm's way; rather, it seeks to preserve peace and maintain their safety. The public pays handsomely for the regular delivery of such a valuable good.

Members of the public can vividly detail those public instances wherein their safety was compromised as their lives were placed in mortal jeopardy. When questioned about this traumatic event, the focus of the conversation quickly attends to areas of causation. The specifics of such horror are made available to the public in an official report as conveyed by the public organization with jurisdiction. Such a report typically provides highly valuable insights as developed by a cadre of subject matter experts. These experts are also called upon to tender thoughtful recommendations of a preventative nature. However, the promise of change that manifests in this and other such resources of knowledge tend to vanish in the postcrisis world.

These items of officialdom often find a tidy electronic and hard copy *home* as they are quickly ensconced in a secure public site. This reality can squash their full knowledge-generating potential; their rich primary data and information offerings remain essentially untapped. The rare opportunity for the senior public official(s) to engage a finite group of world-class scholars and practitioners who can unlock and crystallize the knowledge lodged in such official materials evaporates into the ether. These items then become the long-term oversight responsibility of the bureaucracy wherein matters that were once approached with a sense of urgency now slumber in a bureaucratic regime that regresses back to a normal in which tasks are approached in a perfunctory fashion. The public carries on, unaware that the threat that presumably had been mitigated sometime in the past remains at best dormant. Unfortunately, this type of public service realm places a premium on the precision of action. Such a skill set does not come as easy as it is perishable in nature. If allowed to diminish, then service delivery action and nonaction can have equal, deleterious weight; this condition comes with the ominous implication that could manifest in ways that are best described as *colossal*. The AT manager proceeds mindful of this implication and along with other challenge areas related to the muddling's of the bureaucracy. The AT manager shoulders the heavyweight of this operating ecology while constantly striving to preserve the consistent availability of the social product to the public (Simon, 1962, 2000, 2002).

AT and the Social Product

The key that unlocks the utility and value of the AT intervention resides in its ability to maintain a keen focus upon those attributes of an interagency, problem-solving arrangement that serves as root-cause indicators of the complex problem. The AT manager can then channel attention upon those areas where the interest of the self was misplaced by its leaders and/or its influential members. The illuminated impacts of such dysfunctional behavior can be found to disrupt the activities of those who provide mission-driven service expertise at the street-level. The mission of the organization drives much of the work of AT. The organizational mission is based upon the insights found to be embedded in the work of a professional field(s) as fashioned through years of practice, academic research, and the individual expertise garnered via frontline service. It is in such a practitioner setting that the bulk of the tethering manager's work is conducted and flourishes (as detailed in chapter 2).

In the practitioner setting, a crucial notion of a highly conceptual nature emerges that impinges upon the work of the AT manager. The (public) organization as an *institution* can be construed as an *actor* involved in the interagency, problem-solving entity. This institutional actor embodies the expertise needed to bring rigor to their interagency, problem-solving mechanisms. This transformation helps to properly safeguard the expert design of those services needed to address the root cause(s) of the current iteration of the complex public problem. However, conditions can present themselves in such a way that (collaboration-centric) actions are driven by the self-interest of (a particular) agency leader. Such a situational confluence can propagate the complex public problem that then engenders the AT intervention. The AT manager then must adapt and foster an effective decision-making, action-orientated approach to equilibrate the power vortex associated with this ethical dysfunction. Needed expertise is quickly marshaled to restore the (regular) delivery of those services to the public construed as the wanted social product.

Chapter 2

The Child Protection Function

The North Carolina County Perspective

DEVELOPMENT OF AT AS A MID-LEVEL MANAGER'S PRACTICE

It is no longer legal to dismember a child and conceal the remains from police. Zahra Baker's death, as the death and stories of the thousands of children harmed in abuse and neglect cases, should provide a greater catalyst for change. What does the change in this law elicit as you read it? Middle managers in public agencies are well-positioned and proximal to what changes provide the most benefit in keeping children safe. How then do public middle managers operationalize their expertise to infuse change? This chapter emphasizes the value and initial practices of the Administrative Tethering (AT) management model.

AT is fashioned and secured through those high-quality relationships that portend benefits to the AT intervention work. These rapports are vital as they provide critical moral and tangible support to the AT manager; this enabling provision targets the daily torrent of challenges impinging upon the formation of the collaboration of interest. Bonds, such as these, tend to gain strength over the long term due to such shared events. Of utmost importance, these interpersonal links are organic. Approached with care and consistent attention to detail, the AT manager can nurture these alliances such that they coalesce into a useful expert network underpinning the interagency undertaking. This operating arrangement can then render powerful, holistic impacts contributing to collaboration resiliency and sustainability. The Western-10 Collaborative featured such a robust functional capacity. The AT manager made this advantage real by inculcating goodwill among a set of seasoned practitioners; this condition proved its worth as it motivated the long-term protective commitment to the Western-10 Collaboration due to its provisions of public benefits. The depth of this good reinforced existing friendships and helped to build new ones.

AT is unique because the tethering manager seeks to build relationships that engage the individual's beliefs, morals, values, trust, accountability points, and understand what motivates them. These variables attend to the physical, emotional, psychological, and spiritual constitution and character of a person. The individual who binds with and is proximal to the tethering manager's activities proceed on a path replete with risk. This mantra of risk is innate to the bevy of wicked and complex social challenges typical to the public manager's work. However, the tone of the risk involving the child abuse and neglect realm is acute and must be approached with care. The AT manager must assess areas such as risk and craft a response plan for action accordingly. Finally, the AT manager may also explore ad hoc partnering opportunities and other arrangements as the AT intervention proceeds to its logical conclusion.

Simon importantly provides that collaboration, in its essence, assumes a needed support function for other (core) administrative systems and related service delivery streams. The processes themselves involve coordination activities of the organizational operators as required. Collaboration is a process, in turn, that is delineated by a relationship life cycle horizon. The AT manager has the distinctive advantage of nurturing fulfilling relationships, manifesting in the collaboration process life cycle. The AT manager fostering high-quality relationships helps to equilibrate organizational dysfunctions wherein an imbalance of stakeholder power is at the micro, mezzo, and macro levels of interagency operations.

The iterative activities set forth by AT are relationally centered, reflective of past challenges and successes. The action is relevant to present needs and responsive to operationalize solutions that are not dependent on any stakeholder's approval. Human service systems focus on serving the people operating in the confines of a relationship. AT partners reflect on the actions taken place, bringing the system to its present form of functioning, and strategize relevant counteractions derived from experience and expert practitioners delivering services in today's complex child welfare (CW) cases. Finally, AT has a timely response rate since the collaborative is not necessarily bound to gain approval from actors in other systems.

AT DEVELOPMENTAL CONTEXT

The collaboration process life cycle is adapted from the studies of the family life cycle (FLC) psychology developed by Evelyn Duvall (1962) and gained popularity through the work of Carter and McGoldrick (1988) and Rogers and White (1993). FLC follows the general process patterns in six stages, including environment and temporal aspects, identified as (1) (beginning) family formation, (2) (childbearing) family expansion, (3) completion of expansion (developing), (4) family contraction (launching), (5) completion of contraction (middle years), and (6) dissolution of the family (retirement years) (Carter & McGoldrick, 1988; Duvall, 1962; Rogers & White, 1993). The FLC theory centers on the developing individual in the context of building a family ecosystem. Individual persons do not develop in a social vacuum. Economists and theorists in public administration and business management have made similar leaps to include FLC to explain relationships between consumers and marketers and between actors in an organization. AT utilizes FLC to guide the tethering process to aid in caring and nurturing relationships toward sustaining elaborate collaboration efforts.

The AT manager first applies FLC in the home agency to garner support for the specific change mission. It then expands to the same home agencies in separate jurisdictions (each county in NC must have CPS within its social service agency) with the support of the home agency. In this case, where the Western-10 Collaboration was envisioned, initiated, and expanded to each regional partner.

Sharing the struggles, experiences, beliefs, and moral duty to improve the training and education system for local agency staff was the relational connector (tethering knot) that facilitated the inception and expansion of the "family." The focus on training and practice in CPS fostered a creative and productive space, which was realistic and did not interfere too much envisioning changing the entire system. The mission was defined, realistic, and measurable. The relationships were forged and maintained through trust, valuing each member, and giving permission to hold each other accountable for their part. This conditional refrain resonates with Simon highlights that these relationships, as developed in such a context, will enable the CPS manager to begone to realize that he/she will "find all the programs you need are stored in your friends and execute productively and creatively as long as you don't interfere too much" (Simon, 1996).

The AT manager, as relationships are strengthened, should be able to profile characteristics in terms of strengths and areas of growth. This serves a twofold purpose. First, Simon recommends assigning type labels to personal profiles for a general utility (Simon, 1983). Second, a profile's utility assists in proper negotiation among tethered actors by investigating core characteristics to weigh again and test where rationality is bound (BR) (Simon, 1983). Moreover, as a practical understanding individual or collective change happens when conscionable or unconscionable beliefs are incongruent with a mission. The AT manager's intervention is focused on raising awareness to BR, and simultaneously as the belief structure settles into an equilibrium of new or adjusted trust via near decomposability (ND). Simply put, the belief is stretched or nearly decomposed to allow alterations for consideration, and the AT manager is more than a facilitator; he or she is the intentional orchestrator.

Placing beliefs, morals, values, and behaviors in categories can be perplexing, but necessary for the AT manager to arrive at decisional moments to advance change. The manager must keep in mind people change over time, which is why Simon urges general and flexible assignment of profiles (Simon, 1983). Since public managers are encouraged to use general classifications, are there any examples to apply for the AT manager? Downs's (1967) work in *bureaus* and officers' classification offers a flexible variety.

According to Downs, there are seven types of personalities in public office. They are the Purely Self-Interested, Climbers, Conservators, Mixed Motivated, Zealots, Advocates, and Statesmen (Downs, 1967). Each profile lends insight to identify BR in those actors and predict where they may be malleable for change. The challenge for the AT manager is to avoid ultimately adjudging a person to one of these categories. If the manager is honest with themselves and keeps the colossal nature change is on an institution, then the byproduct of that is patience, intentionality, and persistence. As such, Downs's typologies have been valuable from a middle manager's perspective for relational strategies required in AT.

The purely self-interested seek and obtain positions of power to promote a singular vision. Think about a manager, administrator, or director that has said or others have said the following about them, "it is their way or the highway." Conservators, a sub-type of purely interested driven by security and safety, are loyal and trust themselves over teammates, their home organization, the institution, and society. Climbers, a second sub-type, are driven toward the "next big promotion." Sounds like a personality to avoid!

The AT manager's accurate identification of an actor who is a conserver should be placed in distal positions while a relationship is forming. A process with more remarkable patience must be applied in relational development to these types. AT interventions' aims are to decrease the proximal distance. If barriers in BR remain and mitigating factors cannot accelerate ND through the AT interventions, this type of manager may not fit for tethering. The office must still be respected. Change and innovation introduced not aligned with this manager's vision could be seen as a threat to climbing to the next position or security. The AT manager will have to utilize other tethered relationships to neutralize potential threats of this manager.

Two profiles the AT manager should look for in the group are mixed motivators and advocates. Mixed motivators are value driven seeking to improve societal challenges. These individuals seek relationships to accomplish the mission and are motivated to innovate and change. BR for this profile is often stuck systems and latent change. Profiles with this nature may be vulnerable to disenfranchisement from the macro system partners or the institution. Advocates can assist the AT manager in mitigating BR in mixed motivators. Managers and teammates found to be advocates are characterized as seeking goals to advance the team they lead and achieve success in the home agency. Lastly, they can transcend people and politics. As such, advocates uniquely can traverse multiple layers of the institution's systems to craft clear channels of communication for information to be shared with the AT manager and tethered group.

All managers require visionaries and innovators as well as team members that are able to recognize the details and manage them. Zealots fit this profile. AT managers can position zealots to assist in analyzing policies, laws, and practices to find the details (or BR and ND of these elements) where innovation can take root. Zealots can also assist the AT manager and tethered community in analysis of the innovative project such as aligning with policy and law, implementing the changes, and assisting to forecast barriers.

Lastly, the AT manager may find tethered partners with the ability to strategize for societal impacts in an omnidirectional scale. Statespersons are characterized by two indicators. One is they are diligent in appeasing everyone as much as possible. The second is, a statesperson can think through societal systems to gauge impact. Changes in any system ripple in multiple directions. It is impossible to predict all the positive or negative impacts, which is a natural area of BR systemically. Large changes impacting public services such as CPS require, respectfully so, thorough investigation as deep into the social systems as possible to recognize impact areas and communicate to the AT manager and tethered community.

As an AT manager sets out to find others to tether to a shared mission, they must engage in building high-quality relationships for sustainability. In the initial stages of development of relationships, it has helped to utilize a generalized profile system to recognize strengths of tethered partners and areas of BR. Moreover, the AT manager correctly aligning profiles with operations is essential for sustainability as it places people in positions expressly designed to work with their strengths. It is another technique to mitigate BR and facilitates safety for tethered partners to work through ND.

PRACTITIONER CASE EXEMPLAR

Imagine for a moment if the managers and administrators were tethered through AT when Zahra Baker's case was examined. Collaboration partners discuss the atrocious nature of this child's death, and then work in different directions toward separate solutions. Thus, more opportunities for change were lost. North Carolinians were provided what seems to be just common sense change, "You cannot dismember a body and hide it from law enforcement." AT does the opposite. Tethering's sole function is to unify partners, from the frontline experts to executive leadership, under a specific mission and derive innovation and change mechanisms to improve the atypical operations, which are often stymied by the prominence of competing priorities in the institution. The result is changes in each layer of the system through the institution's partners (local and state).

Each of the Western-10 tethered community partners connects through the AT manager's relational processes. At the center of the relationship is a transcendent message of hope to improve outcomes through sound interventions. The practitioners and experts also bonded with academic partners at Western Carolina University (WCU). Two decades of changes without evaluation to test if the changes produced efficacious outcomes mitigates the concerns and threats of any new solutions conceptualized and adopted to improve the current CW system. Finally, the sound intervention was conceptualized, designed, and tested by the AT manager and all tethered partners. The innovation is the product of years of reflection and research due to its complexity and its systems.

CW home agencies innately incur complex issues based on their pluralistic nature as each layer of the system interacts, imperatives increase. Public administrators are quickly swept under the rip current of competing imperatives and often lose sight of how to meet each one (Martinsuo and Hoverfält, 2018; Richardson, 2008; Shadid, 2018). It is unreasonable to assume any manager or a person can maintain all of the imperatives in a comprehensive view or has the ability to work through all decision scenarios to come to conclusions of proper utility for each (Simon, 1983, p. 13). Each imperative or challenge requires an individual mediation. What imperative should take the greatest priority and it attended to provide assurance the public is served and protected? The greatest imperative in public service then, especially in CW, is simply the organization's service. The greatest decisions should reflect a belief and commitment to strengthening the workforce delivering an essential and lifesaving service. The manager is choosing to invest goodwill and trust in those delivering direct service to keep children safe. The reciprocal affection for the organization manifests in decisions that align with management and administration. However, many tangible threats exist, placing an organization's fitness in jeopardy.

The threats listed here demonstrate a lack of proper sound reflection and responsiveness required to address severely needed education and training innovation to remain relevant and responsive. Among many conceptions and ideas, simulation training was the innovation researched, conceptualized, and tested to address the education and practice gaps noted throughout the last

20 years in NC's system. Simulation training was adopted from the medical, military, and law enforcement research. It stands as the platinum standard for preparing the workforce for new skills in a safe environment before providing services or care to *real* recipients.

AT ASSESSMENT OF THE NC CPS OPERATING ECOLOGY

Public managers can employ reflection to evaluate any circumstance in time and space (temporal and environment). Pausing to step back onto the balcony with close collogues from spheres of practice and academia facilitates an examination of public issues or success by incorporating the totality of circumstances (Krebsbach, 2017; Sullivan, 2020). Presently as the issues surmount in NC's CW system, the tethered community looked into the past and the present facts via research, technical papers, and discussions to predict how the system may behave in the future. An omnidirectional assessment also is the fertile space to design communication and feedback loops to ensure information moves without restriction, ultimately positioning the tethered community to adopt an agile and highly responsive set of strategies.

Local CW Management Challenges

The AT manager collected information about NC's CW system's challenges and pain points from the Western-10 partners. The information discussed here represents the collective reflection and factual evidence derived from multiple sources going back almost 20 years. Frederickson (2003) stated the need to investigate the facts to support the new theory. The list of facts gathered in this section provided a twofold product. The first is the conception of simulation training applications developed to improve the CW workforce. The second served as an "aha" moment, as Simon depicts as an experiential fact in decision-making to change something dysfunctional (Simon, 1983, p. 39).

Changes in the Number of Cases and Complexity

CW cases have changed over time. Poly-morbid issues exist in the majority of maltreatment cases. The days of the "dirty house" cases are distant past. Present cases involve parents that suffer from behavioral health issues and substance misuse, and domestic violence all in one. CW staff face various dangers like drug and human trafficking, parents involved with gangs, and various criminal activities. Legally obligated to go into these homes and scenarios with no more than a laptop or pen and paper, CW staff leave each home visit containing the risk of physical and emotional harm.

In the early 2000s, the CW system changed from one approach that fits all families and situations relating to child maltreatment. The singular approach to addressing child maltreatment complaints focused on the investigation of abuse or severe neglect, which was due to its narrow definition. Fewer complaints were screened under the old methods. Change requirements to expand what can be accepted as child maltreatment directly correlate with the complexity of cases increasing. As such, the term "differential response" came alongside the transformation of the definition of maltreatment. The differential response created a family assessment track to allow CW frontline staff to approach concerns with emphasis on family-centered practice versus "a punitive child removal focus" (Bartholet, 2015, p. 581).

Moreover, some researchers such as Bartholet (2015) and Semanchin (2015) show that the differential response is anticipated due to the absence of tethering between child welfare agencies and other related entities. This situation induced a disproportional representation of minority children and increased maltreatment cases. It does not improve repeat maltreatment as hypothesized. Lawrence et al. (2013) found rural counties in NC experienced higher demands in CW services and struggled to meet those needs. The inability to perform to standard is due to limited available resources and qualified staff.

Changes in the number and complexity of cases impact the CW system in an omnidirectional fashion. Organizations cannot locate and hire fully qualified staff and get them trained and acclimated timely to meet those demands. Limits in funding affect recruitment and retention efforts for economically challenged counties. Moreover, the inconsistencies in foster fit units of protective staff cascade over into the services for children and families.

Lack of Professional Standards

Upon hire, each new social worker shall complete 72 hours of preservice training prior to working with clients in child protection services (CPS). The credentialing training process covers CW's history, an overview of federal and state law governance, and a compilation of service components from screening complaints through permanency services, which include foster care and adoption, how to fill out state forms, and some introduction to the theoretical practice. Presently, there is no test to measure learning competencies. A transfer of learning document is filled out by the social worker and their newly assigned supervisor documenting self-reflective notes on what was learned and what they need to learn more of. The next round of training offered is challenging to access. None of the training is associated with a research mechanism that can demonstrate its usefulness in preparing the workforce. As such, CW staff learn on the job from more seasoned CW staff.

In comparison, other professional accreditation standards that can be construed as similar work require higher standards. To become a licensed counselor, clinical social worker, or licensed addiction specialist, one must complete at least a master's degree focused on preparing the learner to assess and treat behavioral health and substance disorders. Programs leading to licensure (legal requirements vary state-to-state) typically demand each learner to complete 1,500 hours of supervised (by an experienced and certified clinical supervisor) contact with clients. Part of the instruction includes audio and video recordings used in reflective techniques by the supervising clinician to point out strengths and areas of growth in clinical approach, interviewing, micro-expressions, bias, and kinesics. Once that requirement is met, those that wish to move forward to receive a license to practice must complete an additional 1,500 hours of supervised contact and sit for a rigorous test of knowledge, clinical theory, practice, ethics, and law. If one of these areas is not fulfilled, that learner will not be legally licensed to practice.

Promotions in CW agencies are accommodated mainly by tenure, performance, or depth of social equity earned with upper managers recruiting the position. Credentialing at this level outside of the items listed also varies from state to state. The NC system's requirement is a bachelor's degree and years of direct service experience but does not require prior supervisor training before moving to that position. Training once hired into that position is *highly recommended*. Current training covers some coaching employee techniques, raises awareness in secondary stress and trauma, and focuses on filling out state forms and accessing performance data. A degree with a concentration in management is required in other professional bodies, as found in public administration or business administration. Professional management and administration fields require an undergraduate or master's level degree. Going back to the clinical model's relevant evidence, a clinical supervisor typically must have five years of postlicense experience and pass another battery of tests to become fully certified. As members of an organization move upward in a local agency or upward in the state agency, the CW agency, the requirements do not change.

CPS Administrative Decision-Making

Rossi et al. (1999) examined administrative decision-making involving the CPS realm through the lens of program theory. The study examined 18 cases in total, 4 of which were identical, and the remaining 14 were randomly selected from 70 preselected cases. The study found (1) consistencies and inconsistencies (the three states varied significantly) among experts and direct contact workers' decisions to take custody of a child; (2) decisions were affected by services available to mitigate harm and risk; (3) decisions are heavily influenced by prior child protection service involvement; (4) complaint type was not significant; and (5) families that show interest in change were less likely to lead to custody (Rossi et al., 1999)

The study suggests that programs that struggle with inherent assumptions and expectations that are not fully articulated or recorded in policy or law can result in decision-making that is unclear and inconsistent when rendered (Rossi et al., 2004). The study also found that the child protection function under consideration could not be fully evaluated due to the standards being unknown and dynamic rather than static. A related finding noted that areas of accountability lacked consistent administration regarding oversight from federal to state to the county (Rossi et al., 2004). This work outlines appropriate large- and small-scale applications for program evaluation as it specifically relates to the child protection function and its administration.

The decision inconsistencies in North Carolina's (NC) CPS system, as documented by the Public Evaluation Division, the NC Joint Legislative Oversight Committee reinforce languishing systemic challenges. This finding concerns CW screening decision-making processes involving county and state administrative staff; this finding reinforces Rossi's concerns (PED, 2019). NC's CW systems are highly inconsistent in screening complaints of maltreatment. The screening stage is a critical starting point in child safety. It is the determination if a child will receive protective services or not. The lack of consistent training, administrative oversight, quality assurance, and appropriate goal setting for accuracy screening complaints has remained in a state of inertia for years. Inconsistency in service delivery and management oversight can leave the CW workforce confused. The workforce experiences less confidence in their ability to do their work (Westbrook et al., 2012). The shear stress and secondary trauma of the work, compounded with inconsistent guidance and training, increase the risk of turnover.

Complexity in Decision-Making

The complexity of CPS cases presents social workers engaging in dangerous family dynamics. Akin, Brook, and Llyod (2015) stated substance abuse is a prominent link to serious child abuse and emotional disturbances (Akin et al., 2015, p. 83). CPS staff are called to domestic violence scenes and are often the first to arrive, which can prove deadly for the social worker, child, or parent (Agnew-Brune et al., 2017, p. 1931). Untreated mental illness in parents or children combined with substance misuse and domestic violence is a cocktail for disaster (Hodges et al., 2012). Decision-making in CPS cases is not black and white. The wicked nature in which the above elements intermingle creates a distressing scenario for even the brightest and experienced social worker to make decisions pertaining to safety.

The enmeshed dynamics mentioned earlier, coupled with family systems dynamics, promulgates a dense arena for researchers to extrapolate answers to improve decision-making schema. Furthermore, states and local child protection agencies do not make it easy due to layers of federal and state confidentiality laws keeping investigators at bay from conducting proper evaluation (Rossi et al., 2004). It is recommended for scholars and practitioners to work cohesively to craft solutions to bridge this gap. The CPS-experienced scholar-practitioners are familiar with the compounded challenges and what data is necessary to evaluate decision-making in CPS agencies. Research regarding decision-making evaluation to this point has been conducted from an academic perspective (Fluke et al., 2020).

CPS is often the subject of harsh criticisms in the media. Little research is focused on the decision-making and judgment schema social workers apply to keep children safe (Keddell, 2014). Federal and state confidentiality laws restrict the public from knowledge to mitigate a perceived failing system (Vis & Fossum, 2013). As such, investigation into how CPS social workers make casework decisions is the critical question to answer (Maguire-Jack and Showalter, 2016). Moreover, understanding the how, when, what, who, why, and where of decision schema can provide pathways to improving the service and turning the media narrative toward the positive (Fluke et al., 2020). The challenging factor in this investigation is the lack of relevant research to explore. An in-depth search in the ProQuest database yields only 127 articles associated with CPS and decision-making in the last 25 years.

Client, Social Worker, Organizational, and System Trust

Rendering CW services is anchored in a balanced relationship of protecting the child and building trust. A CW investigator has a greater chance of gathering pertinent facts necessary to assess the worries of safety issues if they can at the same time build trust with each participant in the case (Berlanda et al., 2017). According to Downs (1967), trust risk factors for any decision-maker are time and intellectual capacity. Complexity and caseload sizes diminishes a CW social worker's ability to effectively build rapport and trust with the family unit. This deficiency can compromise the social worker's capacity to mitigate existing maltreatment factors.

Local CW agencies may contain numerous other human services along with CW. The executive leader, often known in statutes as the director, cannot focus on one single service. A local agency may have anywhere from approximately 50 to well over 1,200 staff, depending on the population density. Trust in the home agency is contingent on two factors. The first is validation and integrity of work, and the second is extended via delegation of authority of the director. The integrity of work anchors back to the quality of training and education the

CW workforce receives. The delegation of authority is linked to the director's trust in the current state-mandated training system to produce a quality workforce. The sphere of trust then extends in the local agency's horizontal direction and vertically overlays with the macro-level state system (Downs, 1967, pp. 56–57). As such, issues with poor implementation of multiple response systems, adopting a higher grade of professional standards, maintaining a relevant and rigorous training system, and expanding funding threaten trust from an omnidirectional viewpoint. The impact ripples through macro, mezzo, and microsystems. Ultimately trust cannot be separated from decision-making at the direct practitioner's level through state officers. Later in this chapter and a more informative manner in chapter 4, trust, decision-making, and proximity of relationship will be discussed further. However, what is salient is to conclude this threat by stating the further an actor is away from the direct line work, the greater the strain it has on trust and decision-making.

CPS Staff Turnover

Nationally, turnover in CW causes substantive fiscal costs, decreased morale of remaining workers saddled with higher caseloads, and removal of expertise from the organization. These factors have a direct negative effect on outcomes for children, youth, and families. The US General Accounting Office (2003) estimated that turnover in the CW workforce was between 30 and 40 percent nationwide. The average number of years of experience of a frontline CW worker was less than two years. According to Barak, Nissly, and Levin (2001), high turnover in CW has negative implications for the quality, consistency, and expertise needed to address child safety. In NC, turnover has fluctuated over the last three years, with a slight increase in turnover for social workers and program administrators. Please note this information is self-reported by counties. The PCG Child Protective Services Evaluation (2016) delves into the workforce data in-depth, with continued applicability to workforce turnover issues in NC.

Turnover impacts CW outcomes throughout its continuum of services. The US General Accounting Office (2003) found that direct practitioner turnover delays the timeliness of investigations and limits the frequency of worker visits with children, resulting in diminished child safety. The National Center on Crime and Delinquency (2006) determined a direct correlation between high turnover rates and higher rates of maltreatment reoccurrence after three, six, and twelve months. Ryan et al. (2006) found that children who have multiple direct practitioners experience more negative outcomes than children with one direct practitioner.

Flower, McDonald, and Sumski (2006) discovered that an increase in the number of direct practitioners decreases the chances of timely permanence for children. Within the studied cohort, children with one direct practitioner achieved permanency *74.5 percent* of the time, with the percentage dropping to *17.5 percent* for children with two workers. In addition, they found negative impacts on the length of stay in foster care for children with multiple workers. Further, the US General Accounting Office (2003) reported that high turnover rates disrupt services continuity, particularly when newly assigned direct practitioners must conduct or reevaluate educational, health, and safety assessments.

The last 15 years have been turbulent for CW. In addition to the facts pertaining to turnover, the industry experiences a 65 percent vacancy rate within the first three years. Berrick (2018) states exposure to secondary stress and trauma without providing social workers with quality formal and informal support systems greatly contribute to the three-year career life. Lack of resiliency in the workforce, coupled with deficiencies in training and evaluation of competencies, impact a social worker's ability to apply sound reasoning and critical thinking in CW matters across the nation. In 2014, NC was informed by The Administration for Children and Families, the state was in substantial unconformity most of its CW services. Over the next several years, third-party studies from Public Consulting Group (2016), The NC Joint Legislative Oversight Committee (2016 & 2017), The NC Association of County Directors of Social Services (2016), and the Public Evaluation Division (2019) of the Joint Legislative Oversight Committee find sweeping deficiencies of the state's CW system. The largest change can be in Session Law 2017–41, also known as Rylan's law. Rylan's law called for changes in training, education, oversight, and accountability. Since 2017, training and education has not changed at the writing of this book. Oversight and accountability is more than challenging for our state partners that were not granted resources to execute their newly legislative responsibilities properly.

The fiscal costs linked to direct practitioners' rapid and constant turnover are costly to organizations and taxpayers. Estimates for the actual cost of turnover for a direct practitioner position is a combination of direct costs (advertising, time spent interviewing, background and reference checks, training) as well as indirect costs (such as low morale and increased workloads when staff leaves, the liability of the organization due to inexperience and impact on outcomes of safety, permanence, and well-being). Not only is there a significant fiscal impact, but there is a negative organizational impact, which leads to the vicious cycle of decreased retention. The state of NC recorded a turnover rate of 991 CW workers in 2018. Based on the turnover cost analysis (constructed and validated by Marino and Maxey, 2018, based on Graef and Hill, 2000), it costs approximately $111,807.15 to replace a social worker in CW. A total cost of $110,920,000.00 is the estimated cost of 2018 turnover for NC. Our collaborative work focuses on reducing turnover, which causes an omnidirectional impact vector to children, families, and communities.

Moreover, higher than average NC turnover rates, which average 35 percent per year, and a lack of students graduating from accredited social work programs in the UNC system exacerbate a local agency's ability to recruit and maintain qualified staff. The high-pressure stakes of child protection are exposed by consistent failure to meet substantial conformity in the Child and Family Services Review for the last three rounds. Child fatalities strike the heart of the workforce. They have created a culture of fear of the state supervisor, reactive and under-resourced to effectively remedy through much-needed changes in the state's training and practice programming. The weights of the job smother the workforce in toxic, secondary stress, and trauma.

THE IMPACT OF THE AT INTERVENTION

Innovation in training conceptualized for adaptation in CW is the product of almost ten years of research, design, and reflection directly relating to social workers' frontline needs. It is one element that has and continues to fuel motivation and participation of the tethered community in the Western-10. Simulation training is proven to increase both soft and hard skills required to operationalize knowledge of theory, policy, and law (Chiu and Cross, 2020; Thomson et al., 2014). Simulation training addresses gaps in decision-making discovered by Marino and Wright (2015). Reviewing all of the evidence in the reflective section of this chapter all boil down to a singular focal point and increase the rigor of training and job readiness for the CW workforce. The service relationship between the CW frontline staff and the recipient is the core of where all policy, law, and theory are applied in hopes a safe outcome is rendered to the child and family.

Local, state, and federal resources should manifest greater resources to ensure these critical frontline staff receive the priority and focus among all other competing imperatives. As Fredrickson (2003) pointed out, the facts will provide evidence of a theory's relevance and strength through research, which yields its prediction powers. The characteristics and elements of AT as directed by Simon lit the pathway to discovering a relevant innovation to improve training and education and a means and methodology to implement it by mitigating risks of threat from other actors and officers in the bureaus. AT's responsive ability allows the public manager to move in and out of each system with allocated trust as necessary to sustain gaining grounds. Whereas in the traditional bureaucratic systems, innovation and ideas take multiple years to implement, proper application of AT demonstrated the ability to operationalize simulation training in an expansive region of NC in one year.

THE AT RESPONSE

The AT response does not proceed with any sort of disregard for hierarchy or authority. However, the AT manager must negotiate a bureaucratic malaise due to complexity and competition of resources and imperatives (Simon, 1947). AT managers can gain a rich understanding of the historical context of behavior demonstrated through changes in policy, law, and practice alongside categorizing the officers' personalities and interests occupying those positions. Lessons from such reflection are the pieces required to map out omnidirectional strategies that transcend the person and the personality. Moreover, the agility of response is accentuated by the practitioners and academics' tethering to apply sound research to render the accurate weight and measure of response. As such, an overview of the CW system from each level of the system indicates the expanse of reach the AT manager must navigate to create such an agile and omnidirectional response.

Administrative Context of the CPS Function: The Bureaus

CW is the overarching term encompassing the totality of services rendered to children that have been suspected or confirmed to be maltreated by a parent, legal guardian, legal custodian, or caretaker with no legal parenting authority. These services include the screening and acceptance of reports indicating a child has been or is in threat of being harmed by one of the actors listed earlier. It also includes CPS, which is the assessment or investigation of the child's alleged maltreatment (ren). Suppose maltreatment is confirmed depending on the imminent threat level. In that case, the children and family can transfer to family preservation services (in some jurisdictions, this is called "In-Home Services," which is not to be mistaken for similar behavioral health services), or the CW agency can file a petition with the courts to remove the child from that home. If the children cannot be reunified from the removal home, the courts can adopt another permanent plan. The disposition of foster care cases not suitable for reunification can be one of the following: legal custody or guardianship with a relative, adoption with a relative, close family friend, or the foster family that has bonded with the children; or an alternative plan for living arrangement (APPLA). Children that are eligible for APPLA are older teenage youth that may reside in a foster home and do not wish to be adopted have been successfully placed in a transitional living residential home, or meet the legal requirements to be self-sufficient (citation) (some jurisdictions call this emancipation).

Child maltreatment is defined as physical, emotional, or psychological harm *that has or is* happening to the children. This harm has or is being done by the parent, legal custodian, legal guardian, or caretaker. Each state jurisdiction may vary slightly on the derivatives of abuse, neglect, and dependency (CAPTA, 2015). The overarching definitions are codified in federal law mainly through the Child Abuse and Prevention Act (CAPTA). All states enforce child maltreatment via civil court actions. Criminal elements that arise in abuse and severe neglect cases are dispatched by law enforcement.

The CW staff working in home agencies are typically bachelor or master level practitioners. They receive training based on state mandates and certification programs complementary and specific to the complex scope of challenges found in CW cases. One supervisor supervises small teams of approximately five direct service workers. Decisions pertaining to maltreatment must be made by at least a direct line worker and their supervisor. Some decisions carrying greater risk and complexity may move up the hierarchal chain to a program manager, program administrator, or director. Local and regional CW agencies vary in size, based on the number of maltreatment cases that come into that jurisdiction. As such, smaller agencies may only have actors providing direct service, a supervisor, and a director.

NC delegates the administrative oversight of the CW CPS function to the state division. CW division is a subunit within the Department of Health and Human Services. CW leaders and staff are legally charged (NCGS 108A, NCAC 10-A) to provide oversight to CW's county departments. State partners must provide guidance and quality assurance, measure county performance via data collection, and ensure training is available to all local staff. CW state leadership work under the office of the secretary and health and human services. Internal state accountability is provided by the Joint Legislative Oversight Committee in NC. This group of elected officials acts as the voice of the people to ensure CW state laws reflect a balance of legally sound and quality practice to ensure the child's safety.

CPS Service Delivery System

The CW local ecology found at the microsystem layer includes a host of actors. The local CW agency will interact with schools, law enforcement, juvenile justice, emergency response, local courts, behavioral and medical health providers, guardian ad litem (these actors are court-appointed to represent the child's voice in court proceedings), and local government. As the ecology expands into the mezzo system, a local agency will interact with other CW agencies in bordering counties and any of the named partners listed earlier. The macrosystem involves the state division CW staff and leadership who answer to the federal partners.

The US CW system is a federally mandated program. The Children's Bureau Organization, also known as ACYF, is responsible for overseeing all state CW operations and outcomes. The bureau chart below depicts the

United States' system, which is broken down into ten regions. Officers from each region provide oversight, guidance, and technical assistance to a cadre of states. A consistent review system is used to measure performance outcomes for all states. The child and family service review are processes examining quantitative and qualitative variables in CW cases from intake to permanence (foster care) against a validated set of measurable outcomes. The federal officers use the on-sight review instrument to collect the data and score the state's performance. The majority of these actors are bound in their ability to have relationships with direct line CW staff or leadership outside the state bureau. Collaborative efforts are, by default, limited to federal to state partnerships.

Each state is responsible for implementing a spectrum of services outlined in CAPTA. States can provide additional services; however, core services, as described at the beginning of this section, must be in place. States receive funding for operations, which include personnel and resources. Deficits in federal funding are left for each state to determine how these mandates will be covered. Some states cover the remainder, while other states pass costs to local counties and municipalities. Cost allocation is driven by a state's decision to maintain CW as a state-supervised and administered system or a state-supervised and county-administered system.

THE COUNTY SERVICE ORIENTATION

NC's child protection system is one of a handful of states where the CPS service is conducted at the county level. Each county is legally responsible for establishing and maintaining a department of social services that house CPS. The director is the sole actor (NCGS 7B, NCGS 108A) entrusted to ensure CPS are established and rendered to the county's citizens. In NC, there are 100 counties. These counties vary in size and resource allocations. As such, the quality of services is subject to potential variations.

A department of social services is funded substantially via local ad-valorem taxes. These funds account for approximately 54 percent of the total funding. The federal share from grants such as TANF and IV-E equates to roughly 35 percent. The state contributes 11 percent to the operations and service provisions (NCACDSS Response to CFSR Round 3 report, 2015; PCG CW Study, 2016). Rural counties with smaller tax bases struggle to pay child protection staff more than a working wage and provide substantive health care coverage. Urban counties can pay up to 35 percent more for qualified staff. Variations in the pay structure create poaching scenarios for smaller counties bordering their urban neighbors.

This system is perplexing, to say the least. Even at this present time, it is difficult to ascertain a proper organizational chart of officers' state hierarchy in CW. An item such as an organizational chart may seem superfluous to the grand scheme of imperatives; however, it appears to be similar fruit from the same tree of confusion. Complex systems found in such a state of inertia are somewhat predictable and stagnate. Innovation and ideas are lost either in the birth canal or quickly separated at inception, facilitating a constant culture of reactionism instead of one that is agile and responsive.

AT AND THE CW SERVICE DELIVERY SYSTEM

The process undertaken to gather the facts and the story behind the facts is framed in intentional exploration. The CW service delivery system is only one example of the many complex public systems that comprise the conceptual landscape of public administration. To make sense of the facts surrounding the CPS function's conduct in NC necessitated thinking that aimed to untangle its complex conceptual service delivery knot. This thinking was drawn to the intellectual benefits that could accrue through a fluid interchange between the academic and practitioner realms related to the CPS function as conducted at the NC county service delivery level. Moreover, in essence, this new line of thinking facilitated the notions of AT. Lastly, it also facilitated a greater adaptation of Simon's work with BR and ND.

The focus upon the scholar and practitioner relationship was deemed critical to the success of this conceptual exploration. Frederickson guided the essentials of this conceptual journey as he identifies that [i]n public administration there is a special test of theory—how useful is it . . . the test of theory's usefulness is often its criteria in selecting and classifying facts, and if these are accurate the theory will enhance understanding, guide research, and powerfully describe, explain, and predict. (Frederickson, 2003, p. 8) Locally, the promise of such a focus related to the following notions: (1) to craft a mutually beneficial problem-resolution agenda fashioned by practitioners who have deep understating and experiences specific to those complex public problems that vex the CPS field and those the academics who understand how to design research that can comport the insights of such practitioners; (2) to render theoretical frameworks that are built on more precise, realistic depictions of the CPS function is aligned with the needs of those who render its services at the street-level; and (3) to ingrain the realities of the field practice in the specifics of the research design as it is crafted within the dynamics of the academic research process.

The early stages of developing the AT model and simulation training in CW began in conversations surrounding particular pain points in NC's CW system. Marino (practitioner) and Wright (academic) shared experiences, challenges, and opportunities. This bonding period produced a mutually beneficial problem resolution-strategy and an ability to test a more precise and realistic collaborative method via tethering. Wright (2009) emphasized mitigating factors of separate hierarchical fiefdoms "own" a specific area of knowledge (Wright, 2009, p. 17). Sole ownership of knowledge illumines a threat to the sustainability of the collaborative service. The risk of loss of that actor or actors with critical knowledge stands to jeopardize the project. At this stage, tethering the hierarchies to the collaborative arrangements, operationalized by practitioners and managers at the local level, was deemed disruptive due to the formerly stated risk. The perplexity of collaboration requires engagement with the hierarchical officers, and in the same motion, the threat of singular ownership based on the self-interest of that specific organization or bureau must be neutralized to increase congruency, avoid perilous power struggles, and transcend traditional communication pathways to maintain forward motion of beneficial public service.

In 2014 and 2015, Wright and Marino engaged in studying reasons why child protection cases in NC's CW system appeared to be languishing. This study intersected temporally with early decisions by NC's CW officers to implement a statewide practice model. Wright and Marino (2015) found distal relationships between (1) the state's administrative data and local leadership knowledge of languishing cases, (2) acknowledgment of potential legal liability of CPS intervention outlasting legal parameters which infringe on the constitutional protection of privacy, (3) knowledge resource waste financially and time, (4) risk associated with repeat child maltreatment, and (5) cost-benefit of applying evidence-based contact standards which are estimated more efficient and effective. The technical paper was presented to CW's chief officers as an initial step to a broader study surrounding simulation training. The attempt to tether failed. The eventual outcome can be attributed to the notion that those organizational members who attempt new organizational change tend to be discouraged when needed. Specialized knowledge is withheld as it becomes entrenched and protected by a confederacy of certain organizational actors (Wright, 2009).

From 2016 to 2017, Wright and Marino shifted focus to reflect and evaluate the single-issue development approach's vulnerable aspects. Simultaneously, Wright collaborated with Shiner to conceptualize three tethering venues as applied to e-procurement in the federal systems (Shiner and Wright, 2017). This model's application made clear the essential aspects of tethering focused on high-quality relationships, and trust requires exploration and investigation. Moreover, during the exploratory time, Herbert Simon's notions of bounded rationality (BR) and ND articulated mitigating solutions to neutralize resistance from bureaus and officers in hierarchical positions allowing an intentional tethering community to emerge fit enough to flexibly transcend and operate sans hierarchy.

The Marino/Wright AT model proved to deploy relevant and responsive interventions by fostering an esprit de corps among those practitioner and academic actors involved in the workings of the Western-10. As fashioned upon a lasting bedrock of trust, these relationships continue to yield the anabolic energy allowing acceleration and deceleration to advance institutional design simulation projects as construed locally. The final approach of the chapter outlines key moments and experiences to briefly demonstrate their utility. Finally, the model's responsive nature illustrates the AT manager's protective behavior by the tethered community.

CREATING THE POCKET OF PROTECTION

The AT manager will experience the tethered community moving synchronously and asynchronously to protect them as it is critical to protect the local project. It requires keen attention and focuses on the root of the problem and the goal of operationalizing the simulation project. Movement is timed and directed by the AT manager and academic partners based on periods of reflection to *read* the field of play and avoid the risk of singular motion. The Western-10 studied the playing field and deconstructed the opposing sides' movement, providing a simple movement on a complex field. The series of simple movements gained yardage, sometimes in bulk, while others only inches. When the team is fourth and inches from the goal line, those inches bear success.

What Are We Playing at and Why?

The heart of the issues discussed in this chapter conveys into both a simple and complex singular root. The problem is both simple and complex since the subject is human. The singular root is the direct workforce, which is a simple aspect of the problem. Strengthening the skills and abilities of those providing essential and critical services should have the best results in improving outcomes in maltreatment cases. Public managers cannot allow other principles or imperatives to interfere with focus, which is the problem's complex element. Why? Ask this question, "Who is the first person to interact with a family and child in a maltreatment case?" Is it a federal partner, a state CW division leader or staff, a local county or regional director, a manager, a supervisor, or a frontline staff member? The frontline staff is tethered to the mission to keep children safe in closer proximity versus actors and officers further up the hierarchical structures. If sound logic is applied to this or any scenario, the root of the issue is simple. All resources should be allocated to strengthen the CW workforce first at the direct line, then the supervisors that support them, and so on.

Focus on the root. Once it is identified, the manager uses the mission of "keeping children safe from maltreatment" to tether other agents and officers to assist in the heavy lifting of the work. In this case, it is strengthening the CW workforce. If an organization's culture is tethered to the mission, it is clearly defined, and all agency members believe it. All efforts and resources should be invested in meeting that mission. In CW's landscape, where local agencies are tied to the state division to meet this mission, it becomes more relevant to transcend personality and politics to remain focused. Decisions from within the local and state agency should be congruent in meeting this mission. It includes all aspects of resource allocation. An old proverb comes to mind, "You invest your resources where your heart is." Administrators and managers must then continually ask, "Where is your heart focused?" Errant and necessary (discussed here) decisions permitting distraction from the mission generate disruption in the organization's equilibrium.

How Movement on the Field Works

Distance creates more distance. Distal positioning, depending on how far the administrator is removed, leaves them vulnerable to distraction with any number of imperatives. Subtly over time, loss of relevance in the day-to-day frontline work changes how one believes and reacts. As those beliefs shift, the priority and imperative the mission will follow. Currently, as the nation faces the COVID-19 pandemic, there is no greater real distraction. The point here is, managers will always have other competing imperatives (whether self-imposed or mandated by law or policy). At the same time, managers require attention and resources, luring them away from focusing on the single most valuable resource in the organization, it's the staff.

Movement and change are restricted based on the reality and totality of knowledge and experience (BR), and if the system can be flexible enough to change (ND). The state actors' current training curriculum has not been updated outside basic policy changes in more than 15 years (NC JLOC PED evaluation of CPS intake, 2019). Again, the reasoning these officers refuse to adjust plays in the training playbook to improve the opportunity to put more points on the board (IE improve federal outcome measures) relates to findings from Wright (2009). Instead, the current plays are good enough and expect outcomes that will improve without changing anything outside policy or legal updates. When administrators and managers expect improved results by applying the same solutions, what word does that define?

The bureaus' distance and fixed movements will be outmaneuvered by systems built on flexibility, responsiveness, focus, and goodwill to improve broken systems. Simon encourages administrators and managers to look for these opportunities that are fertile for the seeds of change to be applied via these informal communication strategies (Simon, 1945, p. 213). As such, the fit intra-agency of the Western-10 can design mobile plays with varying options to exploit the fixed and telegraphed plays of the bureaus.

What Plays to Design

Conceptualizing interventions and moving them into operation and practice from a lowered position in the home agency and state division is a task requiring others to buy into and invest time, resources, and social equity. The director in this county realized the focus of the problem and granted the opportunity to build a relationship through the process of developing the innovation. Investing in time to build relationships is the first step in AT. The members that become tethered are identifying the mission and other actors and officers to "tie the other end of the rope around their waist" to meet the mission. The second is relationship building follows a specific process similar to what is outlined in the literature describing the FLC, which will be discussed in more detail in chapter 4.

AT management is primarily centered on the characteristic of high-quality/ trust relationships. The tethering manager must on a 1:1 platform tether to each actor/officer in the home agency and abroad. In the NC example, the AT manager strategically utilizes trust, value, accountability, and motivation as the four chords that strengthen the tethering rope. The focused goal or innovation, congruent with the mission to keep children safe, sits in the middle of a balanced axis or equilibrium state. In any organization, this would indicate a fit organization, and this same matrix is applied as the AT manager seeks to identify and tether to leaders and agencies outside the home agency. As members are brought into the tethered community, it establishes a *pocket of safety* for the AT manager.

The *pocket* is an essential fact discovered in identifying the theory of AT. The Western-10-tethered community, by tethering to each county director of the CW agency has tethered to the project. These relationships all contain the four elements necessary to sustain high-quality/trust relationships. They all pledged resources, social equity, and time to ensure simulation training for CW staff came to fruition.

How the Pocket Was Discovered

The conceptualization and naming of the *pocket* come from American Football and reflecting on how legacy coaches such as Vince Lombardi, for example, build talented professional teams that perform well. The team has a singular mission, win. The winner is the team that scores the most points. It is that simple! The complicating factors are in the details of how the points are scored. The quarterback is skilled in knowing all the plays to choose from to move the ball down the field to score points. The other members of the offense have instructions based on position and which play is being called. All highly dedicated and committed to executing their part, and at the same time trusting in their teammates to execute their part. The quarterback builds relationships with each player to encourage trust, value, accountability, and motivation. In order for the quarterback to have time to read the defensive field and execute the play, those offensive teammates must form a protective pocket around them. The defense is any single or set of actors opposed to an outside idea, indifferent, or provide positive lip service to the innovation and unwilling to tether in. Multiple plays can be configured with these basic yet critical actors.

Who Are the Actors, and How Are They Assembled?

The pocket consists of actors working within the pocket with the AT manager and outside the pocket. The quarterback, AT manager, emerges or is chosen within the home agency or microsystem, which is the Western-10, based on an innovative solution to the complex problem. Just like a QB in football, this person has the knowledge of the system and governance. The QB has studied systemic movements over time and can predict how the defense will move. The high-quality relationships built with the Western-10 directors, private agency stakeholders, elected officials, and the academic realm work together to move the innovation forward in their strengths and cash in their social equity.

The Utility of the Pocket: To Create Omnidirectional Movement

Indeed, this strategy allows a middle manager to move in multiple directions through various systems without traversing further up and deeper into the hierarchy of the bureaus in an attempt to find the right position to impact change in the system. Instead, the AT moves the collaborative together, utilizing each partner's strengths to execute with precision timing and force to neutralize the defensive actions or reactions. The beneficial protection of the pocket allows the AT manager to examine the field of play and make adjustments in strategy in split-second timing based on movement in the defensive zone. A final component of protection considered part of the pocket is the "Lombardi," or coach figure, which is the academic(s). The action sequences of movement are tested back and forth with theory and research-driven characteristics to predict how the defense will react. In preparation for a game, the coach may study game films for countless hours to find the other team's vulnerabilities. This knowledge, paralleled to a research review in the academic universe, cannot be underappreciated.

The following event serves as an example of how the pocket provides omnidirectional movement. In late winter 2019, after a full year of solidifying the Western-10 relationships and academic partners at WCU, an opportunity to test the strength of the relationships emerged. State partners from the secretary's office and CW leadership were requested to meet to negotiate resources and strengthen the already established support for the simulation project. The AT manager, the Western-10, and WCU estimating the distal relationship between the tethered community and the state officers required a collective voice to appeal for action. The product of the collective action led to a series of events moving the simulation training forward

AT and the Pocket: How They Fit Together

In conclusion, AT applies facts gathered during the formulation and reflective stages, identifying and categorizing both the characteristics and singular and catholic behavior of BR. Awareness of each actor's limitations and strengths allows the AT manager to mold the team and position them according to specific consensus as buttressed by trust and instituted by key accountability provisions. Much like the professional players, individuals are assigned positions on the team wherein each member accords to their strengths to provide meaning to the newly minted *team*. As designed, this team structure is inculcated with a keen sense pride and motivated by milieu of urgency to attain victory for all.

The players have plenty of space and are not heavily restricted. They know the manual and playbook and also have the experience and knowledge to adjust any steps that (1) protect the quarterback (AT manager) and (2) allow for the forward movement of the play (establishing the simulation project). Public managers seek to centralize decision-making via the manual approach. However, there are always specific scenarios where the manual's adaption is necessary to meet the goals and mission (Simon, 1947, p. 213). Therefore, the Western-10 can contract and expand in harmony, which is the expression of its ND.

The Western-10's responsiveness is contributed to BR and ND's appropriate identification by the academician and AT manager. Reflection and application of relevant intervention strategies were proven effective due to all tethered partners' high-quality relationships. Ultimately the simulation training was piloted and is sustained in the Western-10 region and spread into other jurisdictions proving AT's ability to utilize omnidirectional forces to change a stuck system. Furthermore, it proves that once a change is in motion, it is difficult, if not impossible, to stop when conducted in goodwill. Chapters 3 and 4 consider additional theoretical dimensions of AT as conceptually presented thus far.

Chapter 3

The Application of
Administrative Tethering

The application of the notion of Administrative Tethering (AT) proceeds along a conceptual path intrinsic to its dynamic, intervention-like framework. The conceptual construct of AT draws upon Simon's seminal perspectives of near decomposability (ND) and bounded rationality (BR). These perspectives help to enable a keen, analytical focus upon the effectiveness of those *coordination processes* underlying the interagency undertaking. An implication of such a review concerns the fitness of the interorganizational arrangement. The rationale underlying this implication rests upon the need to ascertain how quickly the organization (or the interorganizational undertaking) can respond and evolve given the inherent peril that a complex problem may engender for the organization. The organizational imperative to evolve is carefully explored in terms of its manifestations pertaining to the Western-10 Collaborative. It is anticipated that this exploratory review, as filtered through the analytical lens of the Marino-Wright Model (MWM), may also provide further understanding concerning the inherent dialectic that resonates when the notion of AT is mixed with notions of ND and BR. This set of analytical actions seeks, then, to distill down the nature of those (inter-) organizational actions and behaviors that tend to portend the nature of its decision-making as motivated by a pending mandate to evolve.

As inspired by Simon's (1945, 1947, 1957, 1976, 1997) exhortation to dislodge oneself from the comfort afforded by the armchair, an examination was designed to acquire needed insights as to how the areas of AT, ND, and BR interacted and coalesced in the field setting. The backdrop of the Western-10 Collaborative provided a useful setting to conduct such an examination. Within the confines of this setting, a systematic investigation was conducted to discern how applications of AT, as mediated through the conceptual landscape of ND and BR, could provide insights as to how the Western-10

Collaborative developed and continues to sustain itself. The details pertaining to the nature of such capacities are examined and considered here.

APPLICATION OF THE AT PERSPECTIVE

The directors of the Western-10 Collaboration have industry knowledge and decades of lived experience. Change is constant in this industry, and often reactively dispersed as discussed previously. The struggle they (we) face is the lack of focus or proximity on root causes. In this case, it is performance failure by the child protection services (CPS) professionals based on the CFSR (Child and Family Services Review) review and horrific stories of child fatality and abuse. The Child and Family Services Review was created to measure each state's performance in areas of safety. permanence, and wellbeing for children receiving child protection services. State's that measure low in performance risk a loss of federal funding. How is performance improved? Change must be addressed at the education, training, and retention level. It is not a question of like-mindedness, it is a question of how to focus such a group on a singular mission when they have a magnitude of other responsibilities. The perspective of AT is that a middle manager can earn the relational equity required to carry a focused responsibility for the group. In turn, the groups delegate their institutional equity, voice, and trust to accomplish such a colossal mission from this lower vantage point. The directors of the Western-10 knew these children and their families lost to abuse and neglect. They read the cases, talked to the families, saw the pictures of the decedents and in some cases their bodies. When professionals are this close to the issues, they will remain close to the root of what needs to change.

The AT perspective served as a relevant, first-step framework to better understand how to prod the Western-10 Collaborative to address their collective staff training woes. Importantly, it was recognized early on that the AT perspective had to have practical impacts on these jurisdictions. Simon, again, provided a rich pathway to approach this pressing concern as informed with the notion of *organizational fitness* (Simon, 1962, 2002). The Western-10 Collaborative responded to their training conundrum by embracing the simulation training approach. While this training modality addressed their ongoing logistical difficulties, this training design also spoke to the high attrition rates of those individuals newly charged to carry out social work duties. Such a response provided the needed assurance that it was exhibiting those traits comporting to the "fit" (inter-) organizational entity (Simon, 1962, 2002).

To properly implement such simulation training necessitated the strategic intervention on the part of a single, key individual hailing from the CPS ranks with upper-mid-level management expertise. Such an intervention was guided by the AT framework (that had been further developed). Armed with a hearty CPS portfolio, this individual initiated the first implementation wave of the AT mantra. The early stages of this engaging work quickly revealed a unique research opportunity. This situation occasioned a chance to undertake a systematic investigation into a phenomenon that presented itself as embodied in the Western-10 collectivity. Capturing the essence of this window to the potential of new knowledge called for the shrewd yet determined command actions to be assumed by the AT manager. This *AT manager* successfully coaxed a cadre of key actors from the local academic and Western-10 practitioner realm to participate in a developmental milieu that may not lead to useful, tangible returns. Ultimately, the quest to develop this cognitive pathway was its own reward for this team of academicians and practitioners.

This (qualitative research) work began with the systematic collection of field notes relating to the intervention activities as conducted by the AT manager. These notes were transcribed and analyzed such that they eventually embodied as a set of propositions intrinsic to characterizing deeper dimensions to the (emerging) AT perspective. The MWM helped to capture and order such conceptual and practical insights. The MWM then served to manage the knowledge that was accruing surrounding the impact of the AT intervention upon the overall maturation of the Western-10 Collaborative.

A FRAMEWORK: THE MWM

The Marino-Wright Model introduced a robust, resilient framework to guide those AT intervention activities that forged the growth of the Western-10 Collaborative. This guidance was premised upon the assumption that the AT intervention must be ongoing to ensure that the Western-10 Collaborative continues to render the (eventual) accessibility of (a highly robust) CPS as a social product (1962, 1996, 2000, 2002). The Western-10 can be construed, then, as a "fit" (interagency) organization due to its capacity to evolve in order to maintain such accessibility (Simon, 1962, 2002). As observed through the AT analytical lens, the AT manager enabled Western-10 Collaborative managers to effectively pilot the operating context germane to the maintenance of the CPS social product (Simon, 1962, 1996, 2000, 2002). The AT manager documented and analyzed the impact of such effectiveness over six-year time period. Importantly, this analysis resulted from its (ongoing) adherence to the standards of accepted qualitative as well as quantitative research techniques and methods (Cresswell, 2013; Yin, 2014).

It was during this period that the AT manager imparted critical guidance and direction to senior-level Westen-10 operators so that they could orient their mid-level managers pertaining to critical import of safeguarding the public accessibility of the CPS social product (Simon, 1962, 1996, 2000, 2002). This action fostered a useful educational mechanism to inform such operators as to how to improve the agility of the Western-10 Collaborative given its highly complex, dynamic operating context. The reconstituted Western-10 Collaborative emerged as an entity that was more properly equipped to implement a (simulation-based) training programming to train a burgeoning cohort of entry-level social workers more effectively.

The pedagogy central to this training has since emerged as industrial strength in nature. From a related practical vantage, this capacity also provided the member counties of the Western-10 Collaborative with a realistic, continuous improvement process impacting their respective service delivery streams. Importantly, such a programming improvement reinforced the fitness of the Western-10 Collaborative (Simon, 1962, 2002). This improved operating capacity enables the Western-10 to more respond to the constant demand to evolve. Such a response capacity, hence, is vital to mitigate those situations that can weaken the ability of the Western-10 Collaborative to provide the CPS social product on the behalf of its county membership base (Simon, 1962, 2002).

THE AT PROPOSITIONS

2014 initiated the systematic gathering of data and observations from the field as it relates to the AT intervention and its eventual, long-term impact upon the development of the Western-10 Collaborative. As the AT intervention process unfolded in 2014, these field insights were encapsulated within a set of propositions. These propositions were then aligned with the implementation phases associated with AT intervention. From here, the perspectives of BR and ND were then reviewed as to their manifestations in terms of the AT intervention process. A set of AT propositions and phases were construed in an iterative manner (see table 3.1).

Proposition 1—Omnidirectional Forces. This proposition considers a force of energy that emanates from actions related to administrative events such as those associated with a collaboration. This energy can be theoretically construed as impacting an associated, vast administrative landscape in a wave-like, omnidirectional fashion in which concepts/variables, such as distance, time, location, become irrelevant from a decision-making, policy, and/or action perspective at the organizational or individual levels of concern. Such an impact can raise important implications concerning the nature and scope of a collaboration from a functional vantage.

Proposition 2—Action or Reactive Activities to Omnidirectional Forces. This proposition calls for the public manager(s) to conduct robust AT management to mitigate the nature of the external force impacting upon the collaboration as related to Proposition 1.

Proposition 3—Stakeholder Posture for Action or Reaction to Omnidirectional Forces. This proposition considers the import of

Table 3.1   **Manifestations of BR/ND in Western-10 AT Intervention by Phase**

Collaboration Phase	Proposition Alignment	BR	ND
Phase 1: Collaboration Inception	AT event –> collaboration scope (Alignment: Propositions 1 & 2)	1	0
Phase 2: Stakeholder Disposition	AT event –> ecological assessment (Alignment: Propositions 3 & 4)	1	1
Phase 3: Collaboration Diffusion	AT event –> collaboration-enabling system (Alignment: Proposition 5)	0	0
Phase 4: Collaboration Mobilization	AT event –> collaboration manifestations (Alignment: Proposition 6)	0	1
Phase 5: Tethering Tactical Action	AT event –> protection of AT (Alignment: Proposition 7)	0	0
Phase 6: Core Tethering Activities	AT event –> AT management approach (Alignment: Proposition 8)	0	1
Phase 7: Post-Implementation	AT event –> post-implementation assessment (Alignment: Proposition 8)	1	0
Phase 8: New Management Framework	AT event –> AT governance (Alignment: Proposition 10 & 11)	1	1

Source: Data from author analysis.

collaboration stakeholder disposition in order to effectively gauge the nature of the omnidirectional external force impacting upon the collaboration from an AT management vantage.

Proposition 4—Collaborative Activity Impacts. This proposition relates the notion that small things involving events/decisions/workarounds, and so on can impact/control large events/situations and raise key performance implications at the organizational, administrative, and/or legal levels as it relates to the functional nature of a collaboration.

Proposition 5—Effects of Participant Action or Reaction. This proposition notes that *everyone* associated with the collaboration matters. This notion is relevant to the area of AT management in that the dispositions of such a collectivity foster a system that impacts upon the overall outlook of the collaboration. An overarching, negative connotation associated with the functional nature of the collaboration can have a harsh impact upon its esprit de corps with troubling implications from both the short-term and long-term vantages.

Proposition 6—Least Path of Resistance. This proposition warns that the wave force will take the path of least resistance at the organizational level in terms of those entities involved in the collaboration. The assumption here is that the overall system, underpinning the collaboration, must be mobilized to manage the various organizational and functional weaknesses of the collaboration. Such an imperative can be compounded if a negative outlook is pervasive among its stakeholders and operators concerning the ongoing performance of the collaboration.

Proposition 7—Thin Line of Protection. This proposition cautions that the intrinsic benefits accrued from the tethering function are realized within the context of a *thin line* of protection. This protection is afforded and enabled by the decisions rendered on the part of a highly skilled, entrusted, tethering manager who exercises rapid cognition concerning when, where, and how to employ those tethering devices under his/her command. Such tools are vital to the existence of the collaboration in that they help to sustain a safe operating environment as well as preserve a stable organizational ecology for such a collaborative undertaking as driven by its mission and as manifested in those activities of its cadre of operators and stakeholders.

Proposition 8—Tethering Mobilization and Application. This proposition demands that the tethering manager mobilize those tethering devices and apply key tethering tactics in order to mitigate the highly volatile operating context engendered by the recent implementation of a useful, proven innovation as produced by the innovators of the collaborative undertaken. Such an operating context tends to foster a division among collaboration actors at the individual entity, stakeholder, and individual levels. This split can be rendered temporary in nature with the rapid, exacting, decision-making expertise of the tethering manager. The root cause of this internal dysfunction is lodged in the perceived, augmented, organizational capacity that emerges during the implementation of the innovation. This enhancement disposes members and core actors of the collaboration to envision opportunities that are unrealistic and fleeting in nature. If not quickly dispelled by the tethering manager, then these visions can render the collaboration as useless and may negatively impact any future collaborative developments as championed by these actors and entities due to toxic perceptions surrounding their credibility.

Proposition 9—Post-implementation Nuances. This proposition calls for the tethering manager to judiciously consider the nuances associated with the post-implementation as shaped by the innovation emerging from the collaborative undertaking. The tethering manager can effectively navigate this ecology with a focused, reflective leadership approach. The essence of this approach will manifest in a setting that will catalyze the formation of vision that reinforces the inception of the framework that prescribed the early actions of those involved with the collaboration effort. This focusing event will enable the tethering manager to inculcate an operating ecology for the collaborative that can be characterized as tranquil.

Proposition 10—Tethering Management Framework Adjustment. This proposition mandates that the tethering manager initiate planning analysis to adjust the nature of the management framework governing the actions that served to sustain the extant collaboration.

Proposition 11—The Ecology of Administrative Tethering. This proposition counsels that in the post-innovative ecology, the AT manager, as de jure leader, will need to marshal key AT skills to properly assess the essence of the many offerings that will confront the collaborative. These seemingly beneficial alignments will likely doom the collaborative as they will promote a "collaborative schism." This fracture will cause dysfunctions wherein an internal implosion will befall the collaborative. To avoid such trauma, the AT manager must apply well-honed, unwavering leadership skills in a careful, strategic, exacting manner to successfully navigate the nuanced dangers posed by the opportunistic, post-innovation operating ecology currently threatening the very existence of the collaboration.

The AT manager will transcend this harmful situation by displaying a decision-making capacity that is fundamentally consistent with core collaborative practices, values, mores, and vision as harnessed by the compelling nature and scope of the problem as articulated by its stakeholders and those entities and individuals who continue to experience its debilitating, unrelenting impacts.

IMPLEMENTATION OF AT MANAGEMENT

As depicted here, the AT manager shaped the eventual development of the Western-10 Collaborative by carefully assessing the Western-10 ecology and designing a commensurate management approach. Inherently, this work proceeded by aligning actions along either the external or internal construct dimensions of the Western-10 Collaborative. Such a careful analysis of these conceptual dimensions enabled the AT manager to effectively address any factors impinging upon the work of the emerging Western-10 Collaborative. The amelioration of such development threats thus equipped the Western-10 with the capacity to provide its CPS-based staff training as prescribed earlier. This provision facilitated the regular, effective delivery of the CPS social product within the retooled operating context (Simon, 1962, 2002). The expert work of the AT manager thus equilibrated an operating context that had been replete with forces and entities who had once successfully impeded the realization of such a needed (training) service innovation (Simon, 1962, 200).

As related to the tethering process, the AT manager properly considered the overall system underpinning the collaboration in order to craft a meaningful response commensurate with the nature of those impinging, external forces as encountered. The AT manager likewise attended to the internal disposition of those individuals (officials, actors, stakeholders, etc.) involved with and held intrinsic to the management of the collaboration. This holistic review strategically positioned the AT manager to quickly mobilize responses to the various organizational and functional weaknesses of the collaboration.

It is important to discern that the work of AT managers proceeded within the context of a *thin line* of protection. The tethering manager deliberately employed key, tethering tactics to mitigate the highly volatile operating context involving the recent training innovation as implemented.

The AT manager successfully negotiated such an operating context and preserved composition of the Western-10 Collaborative actors at the organizational, stakeholder, and individual levels. Any fractures in this entity were thus avoided. This condition facilitated the administration of *their* new staff training protocol. The tethering manager enabled such an innovation by proactively mitigating those instances of internal, damaging conflict; this response helped to maintain a (growing) positive outlook surrounding the credibility of those individuals associated with the Western-10 Collaborative. The AT manager continued with such judicious actions as deemed necessary due to a highly dynamic, post-implementation (of the simulation training) context.

The tethering manager effectively navigated this ecology with a focused, reflective leadership approach. The AT manager strategically summoned the early actions of those involved with the Western-10 Collaboration effort. This action enabled the AT manager to inculcate a tranquil operating ecology for the collaborative. The tethering manager was able to initiate meaningful planning and design analysis to envision a new management structure to sustain the extant collaboration. The AT manager, by assessing the essence of its many operational challenges, avoided a fissure that would have eventually incapacitated the ability of the Western-10 Collaborative to serve as a going concern.

The Western-10 Collaboration ventured into a new reality in which opportunities for impactful growth proliferated involving its various operational domains. These opportunities called for the Western-10 to strategically plan for the inevitable. The critical challenge remained as to *exactly* how the Western-10 Collaborative would move forward in the post-innovation ecology that permeated the actions, deliberations, planning, and critical thinking of those academicians and practitioners poised to begin anew. Immersed in a second round of AT, the Western-10 Collaborative now faced the daunting challenge of involving the totality of the CPS service delivery systems as aligned with and borne from the granular prescriptions of the new simulation training regime.

To actualize the accumulated knowledge from the first round of AT, the Western-10 Collaborative proceeded with care as its actors ventured into a rather complex setting to diffuse an innovation that was once only a concept. This training now rested in the hands of its operators while implementation challenges loomed in the backdrop. Simon again proffers the perspectives of ND and BR to illuminate a guiding path to assist the AT manager to reconcile the nature of such implementation challenges (Simon, 1945, 1947, 1957, 1962, 1976, 1997, 2002). ND and BR provide critical insights surrounding the response capacity of the Western-10 Collaborative (through its inter-agency organizational construct). Such ND insights can then be juxtaposed with the held knowledge (BR) of those managers and operators tasked with the delivery of the retooled, staff training (Simon, 1945, 1947, 1957, 1962, 1976, 1997, 2002). Taken together, these insights can help the AT manager to properly understand the scope of effort warranted to render the new training effective as aligned with those (emerging) guidelines governing industry standards. The manifestations of AT, ND, and BR are aligned with the Phases of the Western-10 AT intervention as reflected in table 3.1.

From these, the nature of the respective, ascribed phases provides focus related to the capacity of the organization (the Western-10 Collaborative) to emerge (or not) fit (Simon, 1962). The perspectives of ND and BR offered granular direction supporting the subsequent analysis surrounding the nuanced impact area(s) associated with the AT intervention phase. As aligned with the AT intervention, BR and ND informed (or not) the extent to which the particular phase contributed to the extent to which the Western-10 Collaborative could be construed as fit. This organizational dimension defines if the Western-10 entity could evolve to those complex problems that they are certain to encounter in the long term. For instance, the Phase 2 ecosystem mediation of BR/ND/AT provides important areas wherein the morale of the Western-10 Collaborative members emerged as key area of focus for the AT manager for administration of a core AT intervention actions.

Notably, BR (BR = 1 in Phase 2) highlighted the need of the AT manager to attend to the notion that the role of the employee within the organization drives his/her motivations concerning decision-making and subsequent (challenging) behavior. If not proactively mitigated with the appropriate AT intervention, then the singular, negative disposition can easily spread to other, like-minded staff, thus forming clusters of low morale as permeated

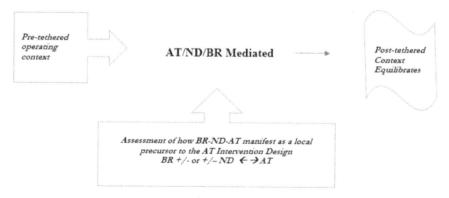

Figure 3.1   The BR, ND, AT Ecosystem Mediation. *Source:* Figure created by authors.

throughout the organization. Such a condition is likely to render a collaboration useless as construed from either the current or long-term vantages.

Ecosystem mediation, in turn, highlights that BR can serve as an important consideration when assessing the nature of decision-making as conducted at the individual level (see figure 3.1). The AT intervention can be construed as having positive potential for the organization. This potential can manifest in those constructive, boundary-spanning interactions between an organization's overhead executive leadership and the street-level service providers.

QUANTITATIVE ANALYSIS

AT is a decision network that forms an effective interagency collaborative process. Moreover, it serves as a framework that combines the Western-10 Collaborative process, staff training, and employee motivation toward an organizational goal. AT utilizes the theory of BR by mapping a decision network construct into a control behavior perspective. Rationality explains human behavior that results from interactions with others following one's interests (Elster, 2008, 2009). By measuring our interest and behavior, we constructed behavior categories by asking what we would do in the other person's shoes (Arnold et al., 2000). Accordingly, we identified that response as the rational one (Christensen, 2016). Herein, we assume that behavior control is a sum or average decision response in a collaborative process without any measurement error (Zhang et al., 2014).

Usually, errors accompany measures, in some cases because one of the items is not assessing what it is supposed to be assessing (Bland and Altman, 1996). One way to ensure that we have good reliability among the items we are measuring is through confirmatory factor analysis (Salehi et al., 2015; Zhao et al., 2017; Speak and Muncer, 2014, 2015). More generally, the rationality of reaching a particular conclusion will always depend in part on what questions we want to answer (Chater et al., 2017, 2018). Sometimes, we affirm a judgment because we have constructed a proof of it from other things we affirm. However, in other cases wherein we construct a proof of something, we already accept what assumptions might account for it. In such a case, the conclusion that we accept might be a premise of the proof (Dubovsky, Gorbenko, and Mirbabayi, 2013).

Factor Analysis

AT relies on BR to implement a concurrency decision logic through a collaborative process (Koumakhov, 2009; Ibrahim and Khaimah, 2009). This is a responsiveness that simplifies the handling of decision-making failures.

With AT in place, collaboration becomes a language that serves multiple and diverse communities to extract the best interorganizational decision-making through staff actions and behaviors that streamline an organizational mandate that continues to evolve (Wright, 2020). These indicators are variables that Confirmatory Factor Analysis (CFA) can quantify (Drislane and Patrick, 2017). The AT process relies on the CFA computation tool to select indicator variables to measure each latent variable. The CFA processes indicator responses into manifest variables that measure the latent construct, whereby the convergent validity and discriminant validity can simultaneously measure different latent constructs (Monahan et al., 2013; Courvoisie et al., 2008).

Forty-four items represented the question's categories in the study. The questions outline the construct of AT and interagencies collaborative intervention. Our SPSS printout shows the descriptive statistics for every item that measures the construct. The interval scale is from 1(strongly disagree) to 10 (strongly agree); we employed the scale to give a wide range of indirectly observed options. We calculated standard deviation to understand data distribution. Standard deviation defines the normal distribution of the data based on the error and variance value to identify the means. The table shows the mean and standard deviation cuts for each item.

Table 3.2 shows four components greater than 1.0 that emerged from computing eigenvalue. The values extended between 1.919 and 6.537. Meanwhile, the first component's explained variance was 38.451 percent, 18.577 percent for the second, 15.461 percent for the third, and 11.286 percent for the fourth. The total explained variance upon measuring this construct was 83.775 percent. This was acceptable because it exceeded the least possible requirement of 60 percent.

Pattern Matrix

We employed the extraction method with Varimax rotation on the 44 items, and we obtained the four components and their respective items from Principal Component Analysis (PCA) (see table 3.2). The required factor loadings, which are more significant than 0.6, were retained. In this process, we deleted the items with lower factor loading. The table shows all the factor loadings for the rotated items are more significant than 0.6. AT, as an interorganizational collaborative intervention, contributes to the process of measuring the quality of decision-making. Our computation performed four components on perception of supervisor effectiveness, which is key to the effectiveness of interagencies collaboration. These components were (1) trust in senior leader's director and board; (2) general job satisfaction; (3) perception of teamwork with an immediate coworker; and (4) trust in a coworker.

Table 3.2   Pattern Matrix

	Component			
	1	2	3	4
SE21 AT	.960			
SE20 AT	.951			
SE23 AT	.948			
SE22 AT	.938			
SE25 AT	.867			
TL39 AT		.982		
TL38 AT		.981		
TL40 AT		.951		
TL37 AT		.951		
JS18 BR			.919	
JS16 BR			.902	
JS17 BR			.896	
JS19 BR			.761	
TW34 ND				.881
TC43 ND				.880
TW33 ND				.839
TC44 ND				.783

Note: Extraction Method: Principal Component Analysis.
Rotation Method: Oblimin with Kaiser Normalization.
Rotation converged in five iterations.
Source: Data from author analysis.

AT involves collaborative strategies that rely on individual tasks distributed across a high-performance team. Perception of teamwork with an immediate coworker and trust with a coworker are inter-related aspects of AT. Perception of teamwork with an immediate coworker and trust with coworkers are individual variables that predict individual performance within interagency decision-making. Aspects of individual performance are relevant to team performance. Additionally, individual performance translates into team performance. Task-related skills and knowledge are insufficient when it comes to accomplishing tasks in a teamwork setting. The PCA computation detects the degree of correlation that is important for interagency collaboration. The significant factors that emerge after factor analysis include the correlation matrix. The correlation matrix between factors has a desirable range of .3 to .6. The assumption is that it should not be a very high or very low correlation, but rather it should be a moderate correlation between variables. At least .3 is a desirable value.

We collected data using a survey containing 44 items. The majority of these were Likert-like items that used a measurement scale from "a minimal extent" to "a very great extent. We derived our analysis from the questionnaire data. The checklist, rating scale, and rubrics are reliability and validity instruments" (Brookhart, 2018). The Kaiser-Meyer-Olkin and Bartlett's Test of Sphericity measures allowed us to establish a PCA at an adequate level (Sig., .000). We determined the reliability of the factors using coefficient alpha. Forty-four categories of questions represented the constructs as a measurement—multiple items combined the basis of factor analysis with a single item indicator.

Multiple regression and path analysis (Khalil et al., 2016) allowed us to analyze the data through the causal model. We also computed ANOVA tests (see table 3.3). Validity is how well an instrument measures what it is attempting to quantify. An ANOVA test is a way to find out if survey or experiment results are significant (Górecki and Smaga, 2015). In other words, the test allows one to determine if there is a need to reject the null hypothesis or accept the alternate hypothesis. This means testing groups to see if there is a difference between them. We therefore limit the category questions to those that will directly or indirectly help us answer the research question by restricting each question to a single idea, although we rely on a few questions that elicit qualitative information. We transcribed, coded, categorized, and analyzed the surveys. The emergence of themes and patterns of response across categories and individuals serves as a further basis of the analysis. We contrasted and compared direct beliefs such as statements of belief or ideas participants use to understand their experience and position with other sources. To deal with bias, we exercised extensive reflection and reflexivity as we proceeded through the survey questionnaire.

Table 3.3   ANOVA Analysis

Model		Sum of Squares	df	Mean Square	F	Sig.
1	Regression	12.006	1	12.006	75.323	.000[a]
	Residual	22.633	142	.159		
	Total	34.639	143			
2	Regression	13.975	2	6.988	47.681	.000[b]
	Residual	20.664	141	.147		
	Total	34.639	143			
3	Regression	15.184	3	5.061	36.422	.000[c]
	Residual	19.455	140	.139		
	Total	34.639	143			
4	Regression	15.777	4	3.944	29.067	.000[d]
	Residual	18.862	139	.136		
	Total	34.639	143			

Note:
[a]Predictors: (Constant), FV11.
[b]Predictors: (Constant), FV11, JS16.
[c]Predictors: (Constant), FV11, JS16, TL39.
[d]Predictors: (Constant), FV11, JS16, TL39, SE20.
Dependent Variable: RECORG.9
Source: Data from author analysis.

In our survey questionnaire, we observed behavior to quantify and evaluate participant behavior, attitude, or other interest phenomena. We therefore quantified the ratings by attaching numbers to the labels, and such numbers give us some flexibility in assigning scores. We employed Pearson's Correlation to test every relationship (Hunt, 2014). The Spearman Correlation tests the quality of the relationship between two ordinal factors. According to Hunt (2014), Spearman's Rank Correlation allows one to examine the connection between ordinal and ceaseless factors. Considering the outcomes, we can develop a value that is consistent with interagency collaboration goals. The principal assumption is that the scores in a single variable are free; that is, different scores do not impact them in that factor. The assumption is that the two factors are of an interim or proportion dimension of estimation, or ordinal to understand that it quantifies a basic and progressively persistent variable.

The connection coefficient (r), known as a Pearson Product-moment Correlation coefficient, is a condition where r = covariance between two factors as Predictors: (Constant), FV11 b Predictors: (Constant), FV11, JS16 c Predictors: (Constant), FV11, JS16, TL39 d Predictors: (Constant), FV11, JS16, TL39, SE20, are the standard deviations of the two factors (see table 3.4). Variables we confirmedthat model variables need not be disregarded due to lack of fit and spurious relationships (i.e., multicollinearity) as reflected in the values of the Variance Inflation Factor (VIF) and tolerance collinearity statics; that is, when one independent variable is a linear function of other independent variables. We also examined the impact of consistency scores

Table 3.4   Model Summary

Model	R	R Square	Adjusted R Square	Std. Error of the Estimate	Change Statistics				
					R Square Change	F Change	df1	df2	Sig. F Change
1	.589[a]	.347	.342	.39924	.347	75.323	1	142	.000
2	.635[b]	.403	.395	.38282	.057	13.440	1	141	.000
3	.662[c]	.438	.426	.37278	.035	8.697	1	140	.004
4	.675[d]	.455	.440	.36837	.017	4.371	1	139	.038

Note:
[a]Predictors: (Constant), FV11.
[b]Predictors: (Constant), FV11, JS16.
[c]Predictors: (Constant), FV11, JS16, TL39.
[d]Predictors: (Constant), FV11, JS16, TL39, SE20.
Dependent Variable: RECORG.
Source: Data from author analysis.

between the perception of teamwork with an immediate coworker and trust with coworkers, which itself is an inter-related aspect of AT. Perception of teamwork with an immediate coworker and trust with coworkers are individual variables that predict individual performance within interagency decision-making. The connection between trust in senior leaders' scores and supervisor effectiveness defines a positive relationship ($P > 0.5$). In this way, the chosen alternate hypothesis would reject the null hypothesis.

AT design successfully demonstrates that changes in independent variables cause changes in a dependent variable. Internal validity is arguably more of a problem in quasi-experimental and non-experimental research, where researchers have less control over the allocation of participants to different conditions on a random basis (Warner, 2013). We use an internal validity checklist, and the measurement of variables on more than one occasion changed results. Accordingly, we utilize internal validity in the absence of a control group in the study measured at the ratio level, which meets the internal validity criteria techniques.

Chapter 4

AT and the Importance of Trust

INTRODUCTION

There are three theories in use when studying collaboration: public values, collaborative governance, and decision-making. An extensive review of the literature revealed a gap in research that examines the relationship between these theories. New research shows they are interrelated and occur in a pre-scribed sequence (Hamburger, 2020). Not only is there a prescription in their alignment, but research shows there is a catalyst that initiates the process. Trust is the impetus that creates successful collaborations. However, it is not a random act; trust is a reflection of value, and value is made up of actions that develop trust (Rainie, Keeter, and Perrin, 2019). Without the cultivation of trust through authentic relationships, the collaborative effort is stagnant, and therefore decisions made will likely fail to meet the mission defined by the group. In the scope of collaboration, we can deduce that trust is not random; it is an iterative process fostered by an Administrative Tethering (AT) agent.

Trust is a personal value, that does not occur randomly, but rather it is instinctive. In the course of any given day, a person will make decisions that they sense are "safe" for them. Even if it may seem rebellious to some, for the person acting on it, they must have a certain level of trust in themselves or the factors influencing the situation. Therefore, at some deep-rooted, innate sense, people are drawn to decisions and or situations they feel can be trusted. Fitzgerald and Wolak (2016) discuss this in the context of relationships between residents and local government. Citizens are more likely to interact and make decisions at the local level because they consider it to be more of a direct relationship. While trust may be lacking they are likely to engage at this level in an attempt to improve the perception of value. This same concept can be transferred to the frontline employee and their immediate supervisors. It is likely there will be more interaction at this level than the employee and upper levels of leadership. Recognizing this trust matrix and developing methods to build intentional trusting dynamics influences how the frontline employee sees the credibility of their leadership and organization. Thus, their role and how they make decisions are positively influenced.

TRUST AND COLLABORATION

Collaboration inherently embodies themes of public values and decision-making. The core of collaboration lies in bringing people from different backgrounds together to work toward a common goal (Cowan and Arsenault, 2008). Each group has a perception of what they believe represents value. The collaborative setting is now seen as a round table of people representing different perceptions of value; however, for the predetermined mission to be accomplished, someone must be able to make decisions. Therefore, representing another layer of value. The decision-maker has their own beliefs but must also consider those expressed in the collaborative forum. Thus, when embarking on the collaborative process, one would be remiss to ignore the inherent relationship between public values, collaboration, and decision-making.

The common factors needed for a successful collaboration trust, commitment, and mutual understanding are fundamental elements to move forward (Chandler, 2017). While these make up the foundation, they are also the same areas that those sitting at the collaborative table have trouble overcoming, as seen in the Hamburger (2020) study.

Wulf and Butel (2017) discuss how formal and informal dynamics contribute to the collaborative process. Organizations with a more hierarchal form of management reflect more bureaucracy, and thus it is revealed in the synergy between information exchange as supported by Simon's (2002) notion of near decomposability (ND). In the essence of collaboration, how invested any one of the agencies involved is, impacts their influence and ties. This becomes representative of the frontline employee's view of their role in the organization.

In this discussion, one theory builds on the other. There would be a void in this discussion if they were not seen as building blocks in the foundation of AT—the organization's definition of public value and how those who work for the organization define value must be articulated first. Value is a subjective factor, and if the organization is going to establish credibility, leadership should seek to reconcile notions of what this means across the organization (Hartley et al., 2015). The AT agent assesses the dichotomy between these groups and develops the bridges needed to connect them. Once connected, there is a pathway between the subunits, which make up the definition of value that members of the organization can tread.

VALUE

In the scope of defining values, the question of decision-making is part of the larger picture. Both the organization leaders and those who work for the organization determine value; therefore, one should consider those roles when making decisions. Jorgensen and Rutgers (2015) stated the concept of value has two lenses, one in which a leader decides what has value and makes decisions for the whole. The second is what the organization sees as necessary displayed through their actions. Because this view is multidimensional, the authors contend that public value is not a rigid predetermined notion; it is dependent on person and place. In Simon's (1962) discussion of bounded rationality (BR), individuals make decisions based on their service role and how they perceive themselves within the organization. This means that the perception of value is influenced by how they see their function and the organization. If they view their role as a positive one, then the value will be rated higher, and if it is seen as unfavorable, it will be of less importance. This influences how decisions are made from core leadership to the outermost employee. Ultimately the frontline employee's perception of value and how they make decisions form the matrix that connects them horizontally and vertically to their colleagues. Thus impacting how quickly and effectively, the organization can respond to complex problems.

Value impacts one's decision-making. In the Raine et al. (2019) study, experiences influenced how people viewed leadership and their government. Individual encounters, good or bad, were superimposed on the whole. Therefore, perceptions of value at the personal level impact decisions one makes in carrying out their job functions and seeing their role in the organization. The importance of value extends across a vast canvas of job roles and personal interpretations. The skilled AT agent is able to traverse this field and develop relationships in which value is nurtured. These are the cornerstones for positive decision-making at the organization's outermost part. In turn, these are the smaller circles that impact decisions in the collaborative forum.

Public value is a reflection of trust. In the research conducted by Hamburger (2020), stakeholders identified listening, communication, processes, outcomes, responding, relationships, and enforcement as subthemes of trust. All the stakeholders saw trust in a person synonymous with credibility in the outcomes. When asked if they could trust the person versus the process unanimously, participants saw this as the same. Therefore, securing trust is imperative in the breadth and depth of a collaborative undertaking.

As a result, public value is the first theory for examination in the prescriptive theoretical sequence.

TRUST AND VALUE AS A DYNAMIC IN AT

Value is a collection of input, processes, outputs, and measures described by Bryson, Crosby, and Bloomberg (2014). When used in conjunction with the Rainie et al. (2019) study, there is a direct relationship between trust, credibility, and public value. These attributes attest to the Hamburger (2020) research findings that stakeholders perceive trust and credibility as organic reflections of public value. Meaning the AT agent must seek intentional relationships that embody the subthemes of trust with the people who make up the collaboration. How an individual perceives their role influences the decisions, they will make within the organization. When these individuals are a part of the collaborative forum, how they view their function within the organization will impact how they respond in the collaboration. People who see their role as one of value will reflect this in the group, which gives meaning to the collaborative atmosphere. A group made up of individuals who have a high perception of their organizational function will embody true collaboration as described by Cowan and Arsenault (2008). When these individual views are negative, collaboration is nothing more than a coordinated effort to solve a problem. Which in itself becomes a spinoff of the individual perceptions.

Trust represents value; therefore, when the employee or resident lacks trust, it influences how they interact with their peers. In areas of low trust, there is little credibility in the outcomes of processes the person encounters. The Raine et al. (2019) research shows that even if the results are credible, if the person lacks trust, they will not see credibility. Hamburger (2020) argues that trust and credibility are unidirectional; when one increases, the other will follow. Because trust is so influential, it affects how the person views the collaborative forum and how they will interact; thus, impacting outcomes. This reflects the importance of developing authentic relationships. Amoako-Gyampah, Meredith, and Lloyd (2018) recognize the necessary reciprocity of trust exchanged between the groups. Mutually important values impact the development of this phenomenon.

Trust is the key that unlocks sustainable dialogs between the community and local government, as reflected in the Hamburger (2020) study. The same can be said for the dynamics between employees and leadership within an organization. Trust is fundamental in how the employee determines the credibility of the organization and their role within the organization. Trusting relationships must be fostered through effective communication, which leads to collaborative forums (Isett et al., 2011). These transactions are an investment that occurs over time; however, they can be challenging to mitigate when they lack the outcomes.

As stated earlier, there is a sequence in applying public values, collaborative governance, and decision-making theories. Before one can embark on a collaborative effort, the value must be defined and secured; otherwise, the collaboration is no more than a coordination of possible services, as reflected by Simon (1972). The Hamburger (2020) research shows that useful and sustainable collaboration does not happen because stakeholders have convened surrounding a particular problem. Rather, it is the result of intentional relationships among diverse stakeholders. In reality, these acts reflect the confidence one has in the actors' relationship (Amoako-Gyampah et al., 2018).

Trust and credibility are core themes that funnel into collaboration, public value, and decision-making. Therefore, once you initiate a properly coordinated circle of trust, there is forward momentum; as trust is distributed among stakeholders, it must move forward. If there is a change in the dynamics, credibility will be damaged, and realignment will occur. How the organization responds to this change determines if it is repairable or lost altogether. In the Hamburger (2020) study, participants were asked if they could trust the person versus the process. Unanimously they responded that this was the same; if they did not trust the person, there was no credibility in the outcomes. And even if they trusted a process but did not trust the person facilitating, they did not perceive the outcomes as credible. These themes were so intertwined one reflected the other. In the Raine, Keeter, and Perrin (2019) study, there is a relationship between social capital and trust. When people lack interpersonal trust, it is transferred to the institution's larger picture, be it government or organizationally, thus reiterating the AT component's necessity. The skilled tethering agent can assess low trust areas and reengage the process among those who succumb to an apathetic perspective.

By definition, a relationship encompasses trust and communication between those involved (Olsen, Parayitam, and Bao, 2007). The importance of trusting a person, how it affects relationships, and administration is significant enough to determine project outcomes. This trust dynamic sets the tone for how people will receive communication or other acts from leadership. If the stakeholders trust the person carrying out processes, there is a positive response to credibility in the outcomes. However, if there is no trust in the person, the outcomes are not seen as credible. In the Hamburger (2020), participants were asked, 'If trust expectation is a reciprocal gesture?' Meaning, do both groups have an expectation to trust the other and the participants agreed there is an expectation of accountability. When one entity opens the door to trust, it is appropriate for the other group to be held to a higher standard. One can begin to see how individual decisions influence the trust vector in their primary operations and within the scope of the organization.

Simon's principle of BR recognizes that individuals make decisions based on what they believe to be right in carrying out their role. However, individual experiences within the organization can alter the decisions that are made. If the employee has encountered negative interactions, they will most likely perceive the organization negatively regardless of their role. This would be reflected in the decisions they make. Likewise, if encounters have always been positive, their decisions would manifest favorably toward the organization. Raine et al. (2019) argue that individual perceptions of their environment can be transposed onto the organization. Thus, these smaller areas of perceived value in totality impact how effective the organization can respond to complex problems. When one subunit has a low perspective of value that is not addressed, it impacts how decisions are made. Now outcomes from this unit influence the next, perpetuating an inability to respond quickly and effectively when problems arise. This gives rise to Simon's notion of ND.

Reflecting on Simon's notion of ND, the organization or government has a core, and some subunits extend out and continue to branch out until it reaches its most frontline employee. Ultimately these departments and people within them are connected regardless of the number between the core and frontline. These connections are energy bonds much like those of an atom. If it is a strong connection, there is a synergy between the units that reflects the elements of trust described in the Hamburger (2020); Raine, Keeter, and Perrin (2019); and OECD (2013) research, and the organization or government can respond quickly and effectively to complex problems. However, as the research shows, when these bonds are weak, the response is slow and ineffective, meaning the problem has exceeded the organization's ability to respond and correct. If the tethering agent fosters trust, they must reflect on listening, communication, outcomes, the person, and the positions involved to properly identify and correct these weaknesses. Ultimately trust must penetrate the frontest line relationships and redistribute these elements for the bond to strengthen. With that said, it is not a one-time action; the organization must consistently reevaluate these dynamics as they are always changing. The skilled tethering agent can make the necessary adjustments, so there is a state of equilibrium.

While the organization is considered the power source, ironically, if it does not distribute its power throughout its subunits and people's networks, it will collapse. In the Hamburger (2020) study, the local government did just this; by not involving the community, residents lost trust in local leaders and credibility in any outcomes. While there was an expectation for leadership to initiate both groups of stakeholders, trust is a reciprocal act. Meaning when the dialogue is open and a positive movement, the government has a right to trust the community for change.

In the depiction of an atom's structure, one particle is considered stronger than those attached to it. This particle would be the organization, and the particles attaching are the subunits. There is a bond that connects them, and if conditions are favorable, the atom stays intact. The elements of trust are always moving between these particles, and they adjust to keep the atom stable. For purposes of this example, the atom makes up the organization's core and all its subunits. If we study one atom and the conditions are unfavorable, the bonds weaken, and the atom can be split apart. Science tells us there is still an affinity for the particles to try and fuse, but depending on the outside force impacting the bond, it will weaken or break apart. The same is true for the bonds between the people and or subunits within the organization.

Next, take the structure of the atom described previously. Assuming the atom and its particles are in a favorable state. The bonds are strong; the atom or organization can bond to a different atomic structure and so on, thus creating the collaborative forum. However, if the new atom is not ideal, the AT agent will have to assess and intervene appropriately, creating favorable conditions to equilibrate. Once the new atom is in an ideal state of equilibrium, the AT agent can begin the assessment between the two new atoms, and the process continues. Individually the subunits are continually working toward stability, and as they merge into a larger organism, the equilibration adjusts accordingly. As this relates to Simon's notion of ND, the larger particles in this description are distributing power to maintain equilibrium, and the relationship becomes a give and take. Therefore, there is a necessary exchange of power between these particles to maintain stability.

Trust is a core factor in long-term business relationships, and it improves social capital. However, it is not without risk; to trust, one enters an individual state of vulnerability when deciding if they will trust. At some level, the person/organization is entering what they expect is a cooperative dynamic. In this space, there is an expectation of give and take between those involved (Humphries and Wilding, 2004). Thus cooperation is the first exhibition of trust as described by the authors. The AT agent is of crucial importance at this juncture because they generate the dialogue and reform needed for the cooperative atmosphere to extend into coordination. As the process continues and assumes there is a trusting state and a willingness to cooperate, the AT agent can coordinate and align individual goals with the organizational or collaborative goals. However, the AT agent is not acting independently. The crux of this process is that he/she is working with these individuals and building the relationships to organize and coordinate sustainable collaborative forums. The final phase discussed by Humphries and Wilding (2004) is collaboration. With the investment of time and intentional focus on building trust, the process can move from coordination to collaboration. Here there is an exchange of ideas; diversity is respected and expected in which solutions and growth occur. It is important to note that trust is the stabilizing factor that initiates this process, and the AT agent fosters the foundation of trust.

Nuances in the Humphries and Wilding (2004) speak to Simon's principle of BR and ND. First, the person entering a cooperative agreement must be able to see beyond their current role. BR tells us that individuals will make decisions based on how they see their role. If the person sees their role as favorable, they will be more willing to cooperate in the scope of organizational growth and or a collaborative forum. However, if they perceive their role as unfavorable, their decision-making will focus on self rather than how their job function influences the organization. Thus the AR agent would assess the circumstances and make recommendations accordingly.

The individual who has a favorable perception of their function within the organization can quickly recognize threats and make appropriate decisions. Thus they have contained the problem, addressed it, and generated resolution before it invades other subunits within the organization. They are willing to cooperate with internal or external sources to mitigate the threat. Therefore, they exhibit a state of ND. If we consider the individual who does not see their role as a favorable one, the opposite is true. It is expected when confronted with an organizational problem, their decision-making will be inefficient and geared toward self, thus allowing the problem to invade other subunits and eventually the administrative core. This person or unit cannot extend trust and cooperate in problem resolution. The AR agent assesses this subunit's state and works to provide solutions for the current state. Here we can see how BR impacts the organization's state of ND; the individual's perception of their role and organization directly affects how they make decisions. These decisions will determine how fit the organization is to respond to complex problems. The AR agent is skilled in recognizing the weaker subunits and, armed with trust, can begin to build the necessary bonds for stability. This assessment is the first element in creating a stable foundation of trust, essential for the cooperative phase of Humphries & Wilding's C3 behavior.

At this point, the people or units in this scenario have reached a new state equilibrium. Trust and those elements that make up bonds of trust, such as listening, communication, outcomes, and processes, are in a constant state of motion. They are continually realigning as more inputs are encountered. Through relationship building, the AR agent can recognize how changes impact the organization and make the appropriate adjustments. This process is indicative of Humphries & Wilding's cooperative phase. In this initial encounter, the tethering agent has created an environment of cooperation in which the individuals involved are open to a coordinated effort toward collaboration.

Trust is the catalyst the tethering agent uses to establish these cooperatives. Participants and employees have to be willing to engage in sustainable outcomes, and this starts with determining levels of cooperation within the organization. Christens (2010) pilots a discussion into the cooperation phase of Humphries & Wilding's C3 behavior description. In Christen's (2010) report, the act of reaching equilibrium is a transactional, relational intervention; there is a state of change at the individual and systems level. As a result of the AT agent's relationship building, the individual or subunit can expand their associations' matrix, which generates new perspectives and strengthens organizational bonds.

The cooperative phase is a cornerstone in reaching the goal of sustainable outcomes from the collaborative effort. In this space, the tethering agent is attentive to the needs of those individuals who will impact the process. The perceptions of value are studied and brought into focus in this phase. There are three lenses the agent must use to observe the context of value and understand the work that needs to be done. First, there is the concept of what the individual perceives as value. Second, the perception of value within their individual role, what their job function contributes to the organization. And finally, how they perceive value in the organization or collaborative forum. Listening is a key element identified in the Hamburger (2020) study and Christen's (2010) work. People innately have a desire to be heard and feel their opinions matter. Carefully positioned questions that probe the thoughts of those actors generate the one-to-one connection needed by those involved. Too many questions present a tone of interrogation, but the judicial use of questions expresses the individual's concern and interest in opinions. Therefore, the actors are willing to cooperate and begin coordinating their roles and aligning them with the collaboration or organizational mission. The cooperative phase is a culmination of traits that build trust, therefore, reflecting value.

The first building block is in place to begin the intentional process of coordination among stakeholders. Stewart, Liebert, and Larkin (2003) outline the significance coordination and alignment of the organizational vision play in preparing for collaboration. Because of the tethering agent's intentional interventions, stakeholders are open to assessing how their roles align to coordinate successful dialogues. The agent can build on the values identified and cultivated in cooperation. In the broader picture, the actors make decisions that are not primarily for self-gain or organizational gain. Instead, they reach a medium that incorporates personal and collaborative goals. Thus, the organization begins to manifest as fit and reaching a state of ND. These are not random actions; there is a prescribed sequence of events unfolding as described by Hamburger (2020). Values are foundational, and in the coordination phase, they have grown beyond personal views. In this space, they have been studied and incorporated to be a new way of thinking for those involved.

Coordination is the phase in which the tethering agent has fostered the necessary medium for stakeholders to become open to working in an altruistic environment. A transition has occurred within the employee's perception of how they see their role. Now, they are receptive and can engage in recognizing how their job function aligns with others in this dynamic. Stewart et al. (2004, p. 317) discuss how aligning stakeholders with a common vision is crucial for success.

> Without a vision that connects people with each other and to the places of their local landscape, the desirable end-state of planning is left incomplete, and opportunities for community-building through civic debate are lost. Resulting plans will be disproportionately devoted to infrastructure development, details without due attention given to community identities that would distinguish one locale from another. Sometimes referred to as "strategic planning."

In this work, the author is describing the coordination phase of Christen (2010). There is a synthesis between these authors' work that identifies the necessity of interventions to reach this coordination phase. Further, the act of coordination is crucial; now, the tethering agent is building on the employee's new perception of their role and empowering them for growth.

At this juncture, there is a correlation with Simon's (2002) notion of ND. In his work, he describes the organizational network and how, ultimately, all of these units are connected. They are all interrelated to some degree, no matter how far out they are in the organization, but there is a central core of power that filters through these connections. With the coordination phase, there is more power diffusing across the networks, impacting how employees see their roles. Thus, empowered, they can envision how their job function aligns with other network members and services coordination. Interventions by the AR agent in the cooperative phase opened the channels allowing this diffusion of power throughout the matrix of job roles. In the coordination of roles and responsibilities, there is a new level of ownership. The properties that fueled cooperation are realigned, and the executive power Simon speaks of is now emitting outward, generating a state of equilibrium. Now the actors in this dynamic are empowered to collaborate internally or externally.

Collaboration described by Ansell and Gash (2007) is a diverse group of individuals who agree to disagree at times to arrive at a consensus-driven outcome. It is formal and definitive by design to impact constructive change or solutions. In many collaborative forums, the foundations of trust are not poured, and the actors' assembly is not accomplishing the intended goal. Collaborations are meant to be a purposeful, problem-solving, and diverse collection of individuals who have a shared vision for the group. Therefore, one can see the necessity of this chain of events from cooperation, coordination, to collaboration. Collectively Christens (2010), Stewart et al. (2004), Ansell and Gash (2007), and Hamburger (2020) identify trust as the factor that provides stability needed to move across these phases. Agents involved in the collaboration must trust their role within their organization, the diversity of stakeholders represented, and the collaboration's vision.

In the description of this process, the tethering agent has intervened at the broader picture's inception. After months of assessments, listening, and one-on-one encounters, there is an evolution of a trust phenomenon that must be followed for success and sustainability. The stakeholders in this process have continually realigned to reach a point of a willingness to collaborate. Relationships internally and externally have been attended to, creating this stable platform of trust in which stakeholders feel they can work together for the group's best interest. It is important to note that collaboration will follow the trust vector. If there is more trust, there is more collaboration, and if there is lower trust, less collaboration. How people communicate will follow trust. Therefore, using the learned skills of the AR agent to generate successful and sustainable outcomes. Members of the group have reached a new level of equilibrium that is displayed in its dynamics. Now stakeholders can engage in a diverse exchange of information that works to solve their vision. However, if they do not maintain this new skill set, they will regress to a different level of substandard actions, and the outcomes will not be fruitful.

At this point in the discussion, the final portion to review is decision-making. So far, the conversation has embodied the months of work by the tethering agent to develop trust among stakeholders. In the collaboration, decisions have to be made about what information is used and how. Thus, the agent is still an integral part of the process. Up to now, the identification of value was distilled in the cooperative phase and was solidified as the next steps of coordination and collaboration came into focus. Hamburger (2020) described the trust model provided the prescribed sequence of theoretical foundations for use in these early stages. Now, this model is integrated into the scope of the collaborative forum. The agent has to replicate these actions among the group so they will exhibit trust in decisions. In the model, public value is defined and established, leading to collaboration and the ability to decide based on these outcomes. In the realm of decision-making, there are several factors that should be considered. The background of each stakeholder, the purpose of the group, desired outcomes, and the reality of expectations are significant variables that must be considered and influence successful decision-making (Hartley et al., 2015).

Within a reasonable person's scope of decision-making, there is an innate tendency to gravitate toward outcomes they feel are "safe" for them. Meaning while distrust may be how they perceive initial circumstances within the options available, they will orient to the choice they think can be trusted the most. In the cooperative phase of this presentation, the individual exhibits this rationale. It continues to build on itself until there is an overall sense of trust throughout cooperation, coordination, and collaboration. Now, this concept is overlayed in the collaborative forum and displayed among the group. The leader that emerged among the stakeholders has been on the receiving end in which colleagues are deciding if they can trust. However, the leader is also deciding how trusting they are of their collaborative partners and repeating the original process.

The emergent group leader has a responsibility to use their expertise in managing all parties' interests to develop a decision supporting the public, political, and private arenas (Van Stigt et al., 2015). The nature of making a decision implies that the person with that responsibility has considered multiple variables in arriving at the said choice. Therefore, the administrator follows a process or a systematic approach to develop a conclusion (Borovic, Cingula, and Primorac, 2013). In the scope of this phenomenon, the development of trust is the stabilizing factor in which decisions can be made and executed.

Trust is the fundamental element in which these processes work, yet it is often overlooked in the larger picture. Based on Hamburger (2020), public value embodies trust and the actions needed to acquire it. Therefore, we can say that value is multifaceted; it is not constant, nor does it have a single definition; instead, it is everything to a person or a group of people (Bozeman and Johnson, 2015). This leads one back to the original thought of defining public value. Rutgers (2015) echoed Bozeman and Johnson's (2015) work by stating there is no consistent definition of public value; it is fluid and takes on the hallmarks at the core of the collaboration. Rutgers's (2015) review began to bring clarity to the elusive characteristics of this concept. By looking at these words individually, a theme arises; the public or stakeholders makes up the core and is readily identifiable, while value represents interests, needs, or wants from this core group. With this in perspective, one can see how it works in tandem with the collaborative process and, ultimately, decision-making.

Scholars continue to cast a broad net that captures the essence of value. Leaders find themselves as the fisherman who has cast the net and must understand this concept for effective decision-making. Grimmelikhuijsen et al. (2016) introduced behavioral public administration, which combines psychology and public administration nuances. The authors suggested that administrators benefit by reflecting on insights from their colleagues in psychology. Because psychology studies human behavior, Simon (1947), in his seminal work *Administrative Behavior*, argued that this is an integral part of public administration study. When one attempts to understand behavior from the view of an administrator or the public, they are making decisions for, they are also investigating the notion of public value. Therefore, warranting a scholarly effort to look into the psychology of what people put a value on.

There is a wealth of research that reviews values, collaboration, and decision-making theories independently. At a closer glance, the definition of each one references the other. Because there is an apparent inherent connection, it begets further study as conducted by The Western-10 and Hamburger (2020) research. There is a relationship, but the stakeholders' location and dynamics will influence outcomes, so what this looks like for one may not look the same for another. However, there is a fundamental connection between these themes. Trust and credibility are essential factors relating to public values, collaboration, and decision-making theories. Once there is a perception of value, stakeholders will be open to collaboration and more willing to trust that forum's decisions. However, trust and credibility are "paramount," as described by participants in the Hamburger (2020) study. Without the tethering agent's ability to foster trust and credibility, the concepts of value, collaboration, and decision-making represent silos that are characteristic of an unfit organization that will not effectively make decisions and recover from complex problems.

Hamburger (2020) found that trust resonated in all data sources, mainly through the interviews and focus groups. The value stakeholders put on trust emerged through administration subthemes, divided into trusting the person versus a process. In eight of the nine interviews, the participants considered trusting the person and process as one. Trust is an overarching theme in the Hamburger (2020) and Western-10 study findings. The stakeholders in both studies referenced a lack of trust between leadership and those impacted by their decisions. But there was inflection and a desire to want that trust. In each research, participants identified a lack of listening and communication. It was so significant they had become apathetic in their roles. When related to Simon's idea of BR, their decisions will reflect what is best for self rather than the organization. If this continues, the organization will not have the capacity to respond to complex problems and will not reach a state of ND. Therefore, the role of the AT agent is imperative. The agent intervenes among the frontline employees or community residents and, through one-on-one interactions, begins the arduous relationship-building process.

PURPOSE OF QUALITATIVE REVIEW
OF THE WESTERN-10

In this chapter, there has been extensive discussion about the relationship between trust and value. Hamburger (2020) uncovered that stakeholders see value and trust as the same. Ultimately if they do not trust the person, there is no credibility in outcomes, and if they do not trust the process, they lack trust in the person facilitating the process. The Western-10 research produced quantitative data and categorical comments. The purpose of analyzing the comments is to determine if the findings support outcomes from the Hamburger (2020) study or if they produce a different review. Thus, reaffirming the sequential order of public values, collaboration, decision-making, and the AT agent's necessity.

The second purpose of a qualitative review of comments is to generate a deeper understanding of the elements necessary for trust and ultimately successful collaborations in the work environment. This part of the study focuses on how these elements intertwine and uncover additional trust/collaborative arena topics. The AT framework depends partially on the home agency's fitness for collaboration sustainability. An exploration of a sample of home agencies in their entirety is believed to point out fit and unfit subunits as well as characteristics requiring treatment. For dialogue to begin and remain sustainable, there are variables important to all of the stakeholders. According to Simon (1962), once the variables are identified, a necessary piece crosses the vertical and horizontal plain, thus bridging the stakeholders represented. The AR agent is the mediating piece that relates frontline employees with other levels in the organization. Understanding how these topics are tethered provides a means for executive leaders, middle management, and frontline supervisors to generate and maintain long-term action plans impacting all stakeholders involved.

WESTERN-10: TRUST AND VALUE
PRODUCE INNOVATION

Westbrook and Marino (2019) undertook two important tasks to aid in cultivating trust and value from the Western-10 leadership down to the direct service staff rendering child welfare (CW) services. The first task concentrated on fostering trust and value in the ten directors which fashion the Western-10-tethered ecology. This task was accomplished through application of FLC phases to appropriately join each member to the AT manager, the academic partners, and each other. The micro-systems work involved recognition, reflection, and action to treat aspects of BR to foster a strong power of ND. The AT manager utilized reflective listening and connected with the beliefs and values of each person and as trust was garnered from each individual, it could then be inculcated into the group. All of which was anchored on a focused mission rendered by the AT manager's emergent assessment of collective voice. As the joining stage (as found in FLC) ended it moved into the expansion stage.

Westbrook and Marino moved to conduct the same exercises with each of the Western-10 agencies frontline CPS supervisors and direct service staff. The AT manager must cull out the time to engage and interact with the employees entrusted with the delegated authority to render services. The strength of trust and value must be threaded throughout not only the collaborative interagency but also in each home agency to strengthen and maximize the tethering bonds. Westbrook and Marino (2019) surveyed over 600 CPS supervisors and direct service staff to learn what training and education they felt they needed to improve their quality of work, not feel like they are wasting time in training, and can see results in the families they serve. Their responses were reviewed and a brief report was generated to the leadership of the Western-10. The answers were ranked in "high priority to low priority" to aid in the decision of what simulation training to build first.

The training topics were finalized and Westbrook and Marino worked from the simulation concepts and assistance from the University of Illinois CPS Simulation Training (to create "as real as possible" training environment for CPS supervisors and direct service staff. The simulation method, adapted from the health care industry, included a "real to life CPS case," trained standardized patients assigned and dedicated to each role in the case, a reflective decision-making tool and rubric to assist in soft skill competency growth, and pre- and posttesting to collect what the trainees learned.

The simulation training was delivered in doses of one week of training per ten trainees. A total of 63 participants with various degrees of experience ranging from 25 years to no experience in CPS were trained over eight weeks (some make up training was required for those experiencing challenges with registration). The proof-of-concept study was conducted on the campus of Western Carolina University (WCU) in a "mock house, CPS office, and courtroom setting." The simulations were modulated starting with the reception of the CPS referral call moving to the CPS worker practicing knocking on the door and introductions, then moving into the home to explain CPS services and why the worker was dispatched, through scene investigation, and concluding in a mock court hearing to remove the child from the parents. All modules were audio and video recorded as a component of reflective learning process and transfer of learning. In-depth feedback was gathered at the end of each module and provided through engaging conversation among the trainee, the standardized patients, and the training staff.

The findings produced by Westbrook and Marino (2019) reveal two characteristics aligning with Hamburg (2020). The first was trust and value fostered between training staff and the trainee. Trainees stated in their reflecting that they believed the Western-10 really listened to what they needed in a training and delivered it. The second was the trust and value the trainees expressed in relation to requesting all training for CPS staff across the state to be adopted through simulation training. The positive momentum created by an investment of trust and value emulated throughout the home agencies of the Western-10 ultimately strengthening the tethered ecology. The posttreatment findings continued to support the qualitative reflections collected during the training sessions. Surveys were issued to training participants at the conclusion of each weeklong session. Four questions were assigned a binomial "yes, no" answer, and the remaining questions were qualitative fill in the blank. Table 4.1 provides the thematic analysis from the qualitative answers.

METHODOLOGY

Qualitative analysis of the sample home agencies, where n = 161, comments is a means of conducting a case study of the data. Yin (2018) argues that the case study method is appropriate when studying existing theories, a common occurrence, and longitudinal events. Each of these areas is captured under the umbrella of a single case study. In this study's review of comments, the relationship between public value, collaboration, and decision-making theories is under investigation.

The participant comments were analyzed using INVIVO 12 software, which follows the same procedures and initial themes as those found in Hamburger (2020). The statements were organized according to the question category and identifying the participant ID. Once these were related, the researcher could easily see comments from the same participant and review their perception related to that category. Organizing the comments also provided a way of capturing the overall view of each participant. Without this step, the responses did not reflect one person's single thought process and distorted the data. It appeared as though every comment in every category is a different person. It is vital to capture the totality of one participant's view

Table 4.1   Emergent Themes

WE WANT MORE SIMS!!!!!!
The Simulation is REAL from the first knock on the door to testifying at the Nonsecure Hearing!
The Court Room Simulation was AMAZING. We need more of this training!
The standardized patients were just like the clients we see in our cases!!!!!
The Class Room was interactive and I learned more about how policy, practice, and law come to life in the Simulation
More SIMS, MORE SIMS!!! All child welfare staff should be trained this way!!!
Where has this training been all my career!!! I wish I would have had this when I started!!!!

Source: Westbroon and Marino (2019).

to understand their overall perceptions and how personal views are related or unrelated.

Because the concepts of trust described in Hamburger (2020) are under investigation, these were entered as the initial major and subthemes for the Western-10 study (Armat et al., 2018). After a review of the data, new themes emerged, which reflect inductive thematic analysis. Thematic analysis is not a rigid notion, and the researcher should be fluid in the process, thus incorporating new themes that evolve as the research unfolds (Guest et al., 2014). Therefore, a more spherical view of the data is presented. Table 4.2 identifies the major themes and subthemes used for this analysis.

DISCUSSION OF THE FINDINGS

AT management requires a keen and sophisticated attention to the details of human expression. BR can be implicitly or explicitly expressed (Simon, 1983). As such, the nuances garnered from what the research teaches on identifying and responding to kinesics and micro-expressions become equally important in what may appear to be mundane to the AT manager. Conversely, explicit expressions of disenfranchisement or engagement from an organization and the thinning of trust are easily identifiable and mitigated by the AT treatment. The findings below illuminate critical spaces in which the AT manager must attend to strengthen trust and value to propel the mission forward. Moreover, in comparison to the task Westbrook and Marino undertook to build the simulation project for the Western-10 via assessing the supervisors and direct service staff, the example themes from the micro-system are similar. This discussion should be framed with two points of understanding. The first requires knowledge of the long-term systemic trust and value challenges experienced vertically between the state officers and counties as well as horizontally among the counties themselves for more than 20 years. The second is the data represented for analysis captures staff outside the CPS departments housed in an North Carolina (NC) DSS The explicit findings of this nature have been repeatedly pointed out by research and technical reports derived by the Public Consulting Group, Public Evaluation Division of the Joint Legislative Oversight Committee of NC, and the North Carolina Association of County Departments of Social Services to name a few (as reviewed in chapter 2). The authors are not surprised to find areas requiring higher levels of treatment as the majority of the workforce were not able to participate in the tethering treatments, and the treatments were secluded to CPS-specific supervisors and direct line staff.

The findings proved to correlate with Hamburger (2020). Trust is a significant factor among stakeholders and impacts how they interact in their

Table 4.2 Major and Subthemes

				Major Themes				
	Safety	Teamwork	Trust in Adequate Training	Trust in Leadership	Trust in Policy	Trust in the Organization	Trust in the Person	Trust in the Process
Subthemes	Positive Negative	Positive Negative	Positive Negative	Communication Positive Negative Listening Positive Negative Executive Leadership Positive Negative Frontline Supervisors Positive Negative Optimism	Positive Negative	Positive Negative	Positive Negative	Positive Negative

Source: Table created based on author analysis.

environment. In the Western-10 study, the participants overwhelmingly did not trust other coworkers, frontline supervision, executive leadership, or perceive their work environment as favorable. One of the survey categories was about retention; one participant commented that the amount of time left was six years or less, so it was not worth going because they were close to retirement. One participant stated, "Since I am quickly approaching that golden retirement age. (six more years) I am quite happy doing what I am doing now for the duration." Many participants commented on how much they liked their job, but the work environment was negative, creating a sense of apathy. One participant stated, "If the upper management can make it a better place to work without strife, downgrading or being talked about to other coworkers from managers. I want to retire from here, and that is my long-term goal." In another comment, a participant stated, "As things stand now with drama and discord, I wouldn't recommend this organization as a great place to work. However, I do enjoy my job." In the scope of this project and study, there was exposure to training. One of the participants who participated in the training commented:

> Today, at this very moment, I feel very supported in my role and enjoy my role. Today, I plan to stay. However, three months ago, I felt very different and strongly considered leaving the agency. I would like ongoing mentorship as a part of professional growth opportunities. In the past, I was told I was receiving that, but instead, I was treated as a dumping ground.

While interjecting the study's retention category so early in a discussion of findings might seem out of alignment, it does provide an introduction into the environment of malaise expressed by stakeholders. The major theme of leadership was divided into communication, listening, frontline supervisors, and executive leadership. One participant made a significant comment:

> The work environment can be hostile, as if your job is at stake every minute of the day, which makes it extremely stressful to be productive. Voicing issues or opinions seem to cause a negative ripple effect that risk you losing your job as then it feels you become a target for a fault to be found in every move that you make. It is like walking on eggshells and you feel extremely unappreciated and expendable to the company. There are few management that can be trusted or that actually listen or care about the employee morale or work environment.

There was a distinct sense of distrust among stakeholders. One participant stated, "The middle management leadership team has not been supported by the executive leadership positions in the past several years regarding implementing new ideas or ways of thinking." Another commented, "There is concern interim leaders bring a different perspective, and their new ideas will be stalled or sabotaged by the DOM." In these examples, the organization does not display the characteristics needed to be "fit," as described in Simon's (2002) notion of ND. Employees are displaying traits that their decision-making has shifted from organizational to self. Meaning the concept of BR is on a negative trajectory for how they see themselves in their role and how their part relates to the organization. One of the stakeholders commented,

> My direct supervisor usually receives feedback and suggestions well, changes are not always implemented, but I do feel like I am being heard. That has not been the case with our Program Administrator. Suggestions and feedback are shutdown immediately with no explanation; in some cases, it feels like retaliation has come into play against those making suggestions.

The distrust continues as one participant states, "Managers tend to get involved with the drama and talk about other employees. When employees have birthdays or life events, each employee is treated differently by upper management." Another stakeholder commented about executive leadership by stating, "They are committed when others are watching; most problems have come from the top down. A program manager position was developed ~~on the second floor~~ because the supervisors could not get along." In this section, the lack of trust impacts the employee from all directions. This participant states,

> Bottom line, each individual worker is not valued. The above is just the tip of the iceberg and some of the most glaring examples. More than once concerns were taken to admin and it's inevitably swept under the rug. There's too much drama and most of it is brought on by inconsistency with management.

This section reflected a love for the job itself as motivation to stay with the organization. However, the stability of the organization resides in its bureaucratic roots. Otherwise stated, if the organization was privately owned, it would likely no longer exist.

Optimism was one of the themes that evolved in this review. There were some stakeholders that, while jaded, looked for the positive. These individuals could also be considered the outliers in this analysis because they were the exception. The exceptional trait was the exposure to specific training designed to address the current lack of trust. One participant stated:

> I am hopeful with the change in Leadership that my opinion will change. I have sufficient training on my job mechanics; it is other duties that I feel training

is lacking. My experience with trying to give feedback is that it was met with resistance.

Some of the stakeholders identified attributes that make successful work environments as stated by one employee, "Or the agency could consider employee training and development to keep employees abreast of software and to better assist our clients. Some examples are Microsoft Excel, customer service, emotional intelligence, and motivational skills." Another participant stated, "I trust and believe the interim directors to do these items, but I do not trust or believe the Board has/will do." Again there is a push and pull among employees, there is a desire to want to participate in meaningful dialogue and add to their work environment, but skepticism remains. In one of the last statements of this category, the participant said:

> I hope that leadership is able to lead the agency to future success. Clear rules and consequences are a step in the right direction. I would hope to answer "5" after a few months. I don't believe local leadership understands the work that is being done in the entire agency.

This participant seemed to embody the sentiments necessary for positive change. They express a desire for change and are looking for a reason to rate the organization higher. However, as these stakeholders have identified, there must be an intentional act of trust to initiate the dialogue. The AT agent is the necessary catalyst to spark this process.

The Home Agency Study findings lead to discussing the sequential order of public value, collaboration, and decision-making introduced by Hamburger (2020). As the comments suggest, trust is the defining factor for successful and sustainable dialogue. Stakeholders believe they are valued when they have a sense of trust in their leaders and work environment. In turn, this translates into work product or social capital. However, to get to the second phase of the model, the perception of value must be secured. The AR agent is that source. In this study, leadership decisions and actions were overwhelmingly perceived as unfavorable as described through the low trust comments. But, in those participants who were exposed to a different set of variables, that is, a specific training, there was a willingness to accept decisions in a positive light. So, there is a contrast in outcomes when there is an intentional intervention that addresses the value phase.

The notion is that multiple factors influence trust and outcomes. Imagine a trust arrow piercing public value is a needle. The line attached to the arrow is a thread made up of factors that determine trust, such as listening and communication. Next, imagine value, collaboration, and decision-making comprise a piece of fabric. If the person sewing these pieces together creates too much tension, the thread will break. However, the reciprocal is true; if the person sewing does not pull the thread tight enough, the pieces will not hold together. As the person creating the design continues to add sources, the thread's tension must be continually readjusted to maintain their design's integrity.

The AT agent is the needle in this scenario. They must pierce or intervene in the values box to generate a willingness to move into another phase. This is a fickle area; too much intervention and employees shut down or engage because they have to as a means of "checking the box," as noted by one of the participants. But if the tethering agent is not attentive enough, the stakeholders will not take the intervention seriously, and their perception will remain apathetic. As this model depicts, these theories are "tethered"; they are inherently connected, but how and what connects them determines outcomes.

The AT manager traverses the thin line of where the past failures intersect with the present changes aimed to improve the organization's health. The delicate movements as described above describe a line of peril in which the objective is to avoid a power vortex (refer to chapter 1) in order to establish or maintain equilibrium and tranquility. In this case, the outcome will be to establish equilibrium by attending to the explicit responses of BR exposed in the data collection above as well as the implicit responses. As introduced in the beginning of the chapter the implicit bias (BR) and responses attached to those beliefs and values are critical for the AT manager to detect and mediate (see table 4.3 for examples).

So the role of the AR agent is one of the great significance. They must assess multiple layers of the work environment and generate solutions. Their acts must reflect authenticity geared toward a positive work environment. In this study, participants were met with negativity at every corner; therefore, anything new will be met with extreme caution. The agent represents a neutral actor who can mediate these circumstances.

There is a process in order to sustain trust that supports interagency collaboration. In the first iterative phase, the stakeholders have to be open and receptive to their leadership. To accomplish this, the AR agent intervenes and discovers what the stakeholders perceive as values within their primary

Table 4.3   Most Common Body Language and Micro-Expression Types Demonstrating Lack of Trust

Body Language	Micro-Expression
Closed, arms crossed, folded in posture	Eye rolling
Pointing body away	Frequent clinching of the jaw
Poor eye contact	Pursing of lips
Easily distracted	Reddening of the face

Source: Jordan et al. (2019); Langdon (2020).

role and the organization's mission. Next, through the cultivation of authentic relationships, the tethering agent seeks to engage the organization. It is a reciprocal process; now, the agent must determine how the organization identifies the individual and departmental roles of the employees. With this understanding, the organization will reconcile these views with the organization's mission. When both groups are engaged, the third phase of the iterative process can convene. Now there is a foundation for effective collaboration that will produce sustainable outcomes. It is essential to highlight that this process is not random; it is prescriptive.

The organization must be receptive and prepared to take in feedback that may be uncomfortable, or they may disagree with what is discovered. But if they are to evolve with the ability to respond to complex problems internally and externally in an effective manner, they must take the prescribed medication.

In the scope of procuring value, the AR agent is assessing the willingness of cooperation, coordination, and collaboration argued by Humphries & Wilding (2004). The process discussed above must occur first before stakeholders can move to the cooperative phase. Value is cultivated, and the employee, with the tethering agent's help, collaborates to determine where they are in deciding to cooperate in the bigger picture. In this chapter's opening paragraphs, the theoretical sequence was identified as a cornerstone for building a near decomposable organization. Cooperation, coordination, and collaboration were identified as another set of building blocks for successful dialogue. These research findings validate findings in Hamburger (2020) and show that foundations will crumble if these blocks are not expertly laid with the appropriate mortar mix.

RECOMMENDATIONS

These studies reflect stakeholders who want to collaborate and have active roles in their communities, whether it is a community of residence or their work community. The desire is there, but they have had too many negative experiences. Their views have become those of malaise and apathy. Both studies uncovered common themes of listening and communication as core trust-building characteristics that reflect value. These studies also highlighted that these must be incorporated with authenticity. Stakeholders discussed that they had not been taken seriously and often dismissed, so they had little reason to believe in the next intervention.

Hamburger (2020) purports one of the data sources were focus groups. There were two homogenous groups: one reflected community residents and the other was made up of nonresidents who had an interest in the community.

The design of homogenous focus groups provides a forum for people who have similar experiences to discuss their opinions openly without the fear of being discounted by an opposing stakeholder (Greenwood et al., 2014). This does not ignore the importance of diversity. Diversity is an important element in the focus group setting because it generates discussion and growth. However, in this scenario, employees are not engaged, and many of them do not trust their immediate coworkers. The tethering agent has to create an environment of consistency and trust.

One of the participants in Hamburger (2020) stated if the local government would host "listening sessions" or "focus groups" and remained consistent in their actions, people would eventually take notice. He stated that there should be a standing date or dates for citizens to come and speak to a representative and that "person should be there regardless of how many people showed up; whether it be two or twenty." By replicating this suggestion, the tethering agent's actions demonstrate they can, at the very least, be trusted to do what they say.

Listening sessions are an essential element because, as the study revealed, people want to be heard. Now, the tethering agent begins to demonstrate consistency, and their gentle probing of conversation among those who attend shows someone wants to listen to what they think. Thus the agent is cultivating the authentic intervention discussed in this chapter. Next, the agent takes this information and crafts semi-structured questions that can be presented in a small, homogenous focus group. At this point, the agent is adding to their authenticity; they are consistent, asking for feedback, and now taking that feedback and generating questions based on what the stakeholder said. This means the agent had to listen to them and communicate to develop solutions for their concerns or discuss how new ideas can be incorporated.

In this study, the atmosphere was inundated with negative behaviors and views from clerical staff to management. Because of this and the lack of trust between immediate coworkers, it would be counterproductive to create a focus group made up of different departments. The agent should host multiple "mini" homogenous groups so stakeholders will be more willing to discuss their views. So far, this reflects the models' value phase and gets them to a state of willingness to cooperate. Once the agent recognizes there is some trust, they can make small steps of incorporating diversity from other coworkers into the focus group. However, as stated in the needle and thread description, if it is forced, any connections will likely break, and if it is not pulled tight enough, they will not engage. This means there is attention to how stakeholders are receiving the intervention, and the AT agent is continuously realigning the trust factors of listening and communication as new people enter or a new group emerges. Eventually, the agent builds this concept outward until the environment equilibrates and shifts in a positive direction. Now the organization has reached a state of ND as described by Simon (2002). The employees' decision-making related to BR equalizes and is neither purely self-motivated nor organizationally driven. Instead, it is centered around both.

In this recommendation, the agent has established value, related it to a collaborative atmosphere in which decisions can be made. However, the process cannot stop. The agent must continually gauge conditions and make adjustments when needed. For example, when they sense apathetic notions, there should be an immediate assessment and intervention. Otherwise, the employees will revert to negative behaviors and responses, and the outcomes will not be sustained. Thus, this application repeats itself infinitely to remain efficient and able to respond to complex problems.

Collaborative governance encompasses multiple agencies, both private and public, and while each of these has a specific reason for involvement, the group dynamic produces a more significant outcome. Termeer and Dewulf (2019) suggested collaborative arrangements are a means to succeed with small achievements among networks, thus fueling more meaningful rewards. These wins result from collaboration, meaning independently, the organization would not have obtained the same outcome. The dynamics between individual agencies create networks that generate a collaborative output (Avoyan, Tatenhove, and Tooner, 2017). These authors reinforce that collectively organizations represented publicly and privately are more effective despite personal incentives for working together.

Zavalloni, Raggi, and Viaggi (2019) continued to expound on the notions posited perviously; outcomes for the whole are generally more significant than the individual incentive that generated the connection. The authors noted that the catalyst which governs or regulates the collaborative atmosphere could be from either the public or private sector; it is the overall results that matter. For growth to occur and solutions to develop, the agency with a dilemma must reach outside of its boundaries. These ideas mean working with competing organizations in a spirit of collaboration, thus maintaining the individual incentive while creating partnerships (Melander and Lakemond, 2015). The authors reinforced the collaborative governance theory's hallmarks, which were a foundational underpinning of this research. The importance of autonomy, yet a necessity to work in a collaborative atmosphere that embodies a governing body, is pivotal; however, this should reflect what is considered public value.

In this study, the recommendation is that the tethering agent emerges or is chosen by the tethered ecology. This official can be from within the public or private sphere as trust is considered the binding agent for high-quality relationships. Moreover, this person should carry a level of expertise as a practitioner in the realm in which treatment is being provided via AT. Furthermore, the AT manager should be tethered to an academic stakeholder to provide the scholar-practitioner interventions aimed at working to incorporate the real-life experiences of the practitioners and sound scientific methodologies. Complex government organizations are fickle in nature and often are not approachable from the outside private sector to puncture the inner circles effectively.

CONCLUSION

The order in which these theories work is essential. There is a sequence in their application: public values, collaborative governance, and decision-making. The outcomes showed that the stakeholder has to have trust before collaborating and believing in a credible decision or results from that forum. Trust and credibility are the fundamentals that tether these theories; however, there is a balance in how they are bound. The findings showed that employees and leadership operate in silos without the crucial elements of trust and credibility. The results further revealed that AR interventions (Wright, 2009) are necessary for sustainable covalent bonds between public values, collaborative governance, and decision-making theories.

The home agency sample survey comments identified an interdependence that lays a foundation for more research; a future research design that focuses on these specific bonds of trust elements would add to existing literature and success. There is an organizational power described by Simon through leadership that must exhibit characteristics of trust. Leadership has to initiate avenues that generate trust among employees so that this power can be diffused into these connections. Now the networks, as described in Simon's work, are healthier and more sustainable. Ultimately, employees look to their leadership to set the tone for a collaborative environment. When the leader is attentive and nurtures these relationships, employees perceive a higher level of trust, therefore, improving the work environment.

The data explored in this chapter render a compelling argument that trust is the nucleus of relationship and relationship is essential for tethering a collaborative ecology. Findings in the micro-system must be explored through the macro-system to gain a better understanding of the quality of trust that currently exists between the home agencies in all 100 counties in NC and the state governance bureau. The findings of such a colossal project are hypothesized to unveil the same characteristics of BR that require palliative treatment to foster greater capacity of ND to undergird large-scale projects necessary to expand statewide. AT provides the architecture of a fit collaborative ecology and the data supports such. The direct process and treatment techniques explored in the following chapter unpack prolific steps and stages operationalized to foster value and trust.

Chapter 5

AT and the Decision-Making Process

INTRODUCTION

It is somewhat paralyzing to stop and think about the factors influencing decision-making. The twenty-first century has ushered in a tsunami of information stimuli via the Internet's viral effects and having 24/7/365 access. New colloquialisms have been created, such as FMO (fear of missing out), to express both joyful and tedious experiences in our languages. While the bombardment or wealth (depending on how one feels that day) of information provides constant access, it also creates a chasm of one's ability to properly attend to a few or one item at a time. AT applies the careful study of decision-making in the child welfare (CW) ecologies to fabricate the soundness of both relationships and the simulation training product.

Why is decision-making so important in the AT framework? This question may not even require to ask some. Think back to chapter 2 and your experiences as a middle manager. How often does change become stuck when answers to complex questions are much simpler in nature? Decisions are often the root of slow or no change. Go back to how the chain reaction started with the federal review of one state's CW system tipped the dominos of information over. The state's CW institution received lists of deficiencies from the local county agencies up through legislative governance. "Hence the wealth of information creates a poverty of attention" (Simon, n.d.). The first rational for decision-making requires keen attention as the wealth of information must be sifted, managed, and prioritized. Second, as the wealth of information induces a poverty of attention, a tethered ecology can apply a decision model to prioritize root causes and solutions versus being driven by the tyranny of the crisis of the day.

One of the major objections raised when analyzing decision-making of an institution, such as CW, is that it is mainly derived from systematic and logical processes (Simon, 1945 p.129). Organizational and institutional behavior in CW is too often driven by crisis and reactivity. As such, we must also consider the emotional aspects of the decision process. There may be many examples that come to mind where stakeholders have decided or the perception manifests that an interested person or group makes decisions to change the institution or an organization through emotion. Decisions formulated from emotion continue to drive reactive and crisis responses, which do not freely permit proper application of logic (Ghadiri, Habermacher, & Peters, 2013; Zak,2017). Our decision choices are then to wait on a study to produce results (logic) or to respond from the peril of injustice emotively as stated earlier in chapter 2.

Zahra's case, along with so many children lost to abuse, and neglect are not strong enough catalysts to change decisions in how the CW institution functions or singular CW organizations. The change experienced by the institution regarding Zahra's case was emotive and lacked little engagement of systemic logic as evidenced by the criminal statute change for law enforcement. What benefit is this to child protective services (CPS) professionals? Then there is the case of Rylan Ott. Rylan's case is tragic and developed during several dominos falling in NC's CW system. Rylan was a three-year-old boy who was just returned to his mother from foster care. Rylan was left unsupervised, and he wandered a half-mile to an adjoining property, fell into a pond and drowned. The response to Rylan's loss was both emotive and logical. Rylan's guardian ad-litem (a person that is appointed by the court to serve in the best interest of the child) acted in both goodwill and out of devastation by Rylan's loss going to media sources, board meetings, and asking for drastically needed changes to the institution. New studies were called for by the state legislative members, and NCDHHS, and a collaboration of county CW directors, county commissioners, state legislators, university experts, and NCDHHS staff met to examine institutional changes. All these like-minded professionals must have been able to create changes to improve education and training for CPS professionals, right? The only change produced was a new law outlining stricter oversight NCDHHS was to provide to the county CW organizations. Injustice often guides public managers away from the solutions that can wrought stronger change. While there are several variables to consider in Rylan's case, what should stand out more than the others is the need to address the education and training issues for CPS professionals. Instead, the cry for justice removes CPS professionals from some offices of service and legislates state leadership to do a better job.

What about improving CW workforce knowledge, skills, raising recruitment standards, pay standards, and retention efforts that the former studies recommend improving the institution? These elements can be found in sections of the law, and in the evaluations produced by the various studies for North Carolina. Rylan's law went into effect in 2017. Four years later the institution continues to suffer from 30 percent to 40 percent turnover, lack of qualified candidates for the job, and a poorly compensated, educated, trained specialized workforce to keep children safe. The decisions and fruit of such point to an unfit institution. As such, a continuation to derive change from either emotion or logic does not promulgate change at the right place. The only decision that is both logical and emotionally fit is improving the CW workforce. All the evidence for change points to this. So, why is the decision to improve the education and training of CPS professionals not being made?

Part of the answer lies in the bounded rationality (BR) of the institution, which lacks internal or external anabolic catalysts required to heal from cognitive and emotive overloading. An institution that remains in crisis and reaction only knows to believe crisis is normal and reactivity is a way of professional life (Simon, 1982). Even if the institution recognizes from time to time, it is unfit due to this type of condition, it takes extraordinary treatments to begin the healing process. Public managers must keep in mind that all the actors and participants in each system of decision-making in an institution such as CPS are impacted and stymied by the cognitive and emotive overload constraining its ability to shift to a position of adaptability (near decomposability [ND]—because we want to address the core belief behind the decision and behavior) to identify the simple solutions such as training and education that will have a greater impact on the system. Moreover, state managers in CPS, outside stakeholders interesting with CPS, and often executive leaders in local CPS agencies are too distal from the daily work, which fosters BR.

A second part of the answer is that since the institution lives in constant crisis, it is focused on the symptoms of the problem and not the root. Stakeholders that view the CPS institution from the outside, whom often have the ability to change laws, perceive the leadership is disorganized, unfocused, and do not have required skills to effectively manage change (cite). A constant state of crisis also lends the institution impotent as the leadership struggles with self-preservation and constant turnover in their own ranks (Benbenishty et al., 2015; Klienig, 1996). The deficits in workforce education, skill, and training were not startling discoveries for those with experience. Cases that end in fatality are always examined postmortem. CPS institutions should have a collection of findings to use to create changes aimed at preventing further fatalities. Professionals that review fatality cases must try to do two things. The first is to review the case documents to determine if policy and law were followed and attempt to place themselves back in time—in the mind of that CPS worker and that team to assess the decisions that were made, and why they were made. So, we are brought right back to the root—decision-making. How do we improve decision-making? Improving decision-making is accomplished through tethering high-quality relationships with the body of knowledge and policy guiding CPS decisions. It then extends into cultivating fit local CPS organizations and then stretches to the institution itself. Changing the institution from a reactive crisis-driven machine that eats itself, to one of health and response is then accomplished through right relationships tethered the body of knowledge and policies that guide decision-making, and with professionals that do the work. As such, the managers that are relevantly connected with the body of knowledge, law and policy, and the people doing the work can act as an anabolic catalyst to change decisions toward focusing on a root problem and using collaborative networks to span the institution.

Skillful decision-making and judgment in complex management systems, including CW, are gaining the attention of researchers. Simon encourages public managers to use logic (administrative data) and human intuition (Simon, 1947). The omnidirectional sources of information required to distill and render safe assessments of vulnerable children make the nature of the work dense. Input/output and tracing are two favorable methodologies applied in the study of CW decision-making (Fluke, et al., 2020; Rossi, 2004). The input/output method collects administrative data from the National Child Abuse and Neglect Data System (NCANDS), individual state systems, and case file information such as scores on safety, risk assessments tools, timeframe a CW social worker responded, and case disposition. Data collected from any combination of the listed systems are viable for any correlation, ANOVA, regression, or factor analysis. The application of certain logic will not account for the countless variables existing in the human worker, stakeholder, or service recipient (Gigerenzer, 2013). As such, tracing pathways of human intuition (or heuristics) via direct application of Simon's notions of BR and ND provide an omnidirectional point of view for fit decisions of the organization and institution. Recognition through studying the cases mentioned in this book along with results, or lack of results stimulated the genesis of AT, simulation training, and practical applications for middle managers to be a catalyst for change.

Defining professional or skillful decision-making is somewhat limited based on the precondition of the rationale of those experts or academics rendering it. The allusiveness of unearthing a specific standard is convoluted by the stimuli of the process generation LEAN Six-Sigma, Total Quality Management, Implementation Science, and other boxed solutions in fad at the moment (Andersson, Eriksson, and Torstensson, 2006; Rochefort, 2019; Sloan, 2017). In and of themselves, these are exemplary methods detaining much of the management world. Any attempt to make such solutions a one size fits all are grave missteps. Fluke et al. (2020) postulated that decision-making in the CW context is done in an ecology. Fluke's decision ecology model contains the CPS worker, their organization, and external stakeholders as influencers of decisions. Simon (1947 p. 305) would agree with Fluke and add individuals making decisions often reflect on how others will interpret it. As such, it depicts the indispensable coalescence between interactive relationships and cognitive and affective processing as used in the AT model applications to arrive at fit decisions.

This chapter furnishes the attributes of building high-quality relationships and decision-tracing. The art and science of constructing and applying these tools offer agility to public managers seeking to bolster or engage in new collaborative constructs. Chapter 2 introduced Downs's typologies, family life cycle (FLC), and decision-making schemas. The target here is to issue how each of these attributes confluently shapes the Marino-Wright Model (MWM) of AT, which calcified the Western-10 Collaborative.

DOWNS AND FAMILY LIFE CYCLE

Simon (1947) counsels public administrators when contemplating collaboration, and it must balance utility and honor human dignity in relationships. The figure below serves as a guide for public managers concerning the relationship-building process. The following section plots out the cycle of building relationships, establishing stakeholders fit for collaborative work, and its renewable energy source. AT is sustained through alignment and focus on the singular mission of the complex social issue, building relationships tethered by high trust, value of the individual(s), hoding one another accountable, which produces motivation for change.

Phase 1: Collaboration Inception/Beginning the Family

The AT manager explores potential relationships, from established to acquaintances, speculating interest in engaging a social change initiative. Initial attraction stems from the shared experiences, values, culture, and beliefs ensconced in those indelible life markers that attend to one's understanding of the world. It is the art of learning and assessing compatibility for long-term relationships humankind has intrinsically exercised for thousands of years. The forming and joining stage are accentuated through direct application of BR by the AT manager. Detection and awareness of rational limitations coupled with understanding how to help another person stretch their ability and beliefs reasonably is the foundation of a tethered bond.

The joining and forming stages of a relationship benefit from some knowledge of personality types and interpersonal interests. Looking back at Downs's typologies (see chapter 2), for example, as the AT manager began to engage with each of the Western-10 CW agency directors, all of them aligned more so with the *mixed-motivated* spectrum. The AT manager found the same in the academic stakeholders at Western Carolina University (WCU). Marino and Wright follow suit.

It is uncertain at this moment if this typology plays a significant role in the MWM. What is certain is the forming and joining stage for the Western-10 was anchored on the vision of improving the resilience and resources for the workforce. All values, beliefs, culture, and experiences of each stakeholder melded through agreements in the shared vision. The coalescence allows each manager to feel safe to give and receive feedback, which is the treatment to mitigating the limitations of BR. In doing so, tethering to each of the executive leaders a kinetic wave of energy poised act and react to external forces.

As the AT manager moved out from the western region's mesosystem and into the state's macro system, this pattern changed. State leadership in CW appeared to fit into conserver or statesmen types. Conservers and statesmen often engage those agents from outside their circle in power struggles. Conservers covet power and control suiting their self-serving interests. Statesmen working for conservers tend to generate good ideas and solutions, however, are not given the resources required to fully implement it (Downs, 1967). The AT manager keenly notes through brief interactions with these officers how their rationality will be bonded. Conservers will seek to gain standing and prestige in any innovation brought to this level. Statesmen may waffle in ambivalence rendering them stuck deciding who they should appease. The AT manager attends to attachments with these officers diplomatically and distally.

Phase 2: Stakeholder Disposition/Family Expansion

In Phase 2 a smaller nucleic group of approximately 2–5 members continues the arduous task to examine areas of growth. A deeper level of trust and value is placed in the AT manager and the direct fruit manifests in the delegation of authority to lead and guide the tethered community. This process of analyzing the disposition of each tethered member catalogs the authority they are willing to pass along to the AT manager as well as what position they will occupy in the field of strategy. Focus on attributes of BR and ND in this phase should yield such results when properly attended symmetrically as trust and value are cultivated.

The AT manager emerges with new abilities and permissions to traverse in any direction necessary scaling hierarchical platforms operating out of sans hierarchy. The relationships in the nucleus reach maturity and they are prepared to multiply. Continually and simultaneously collective impact of the tethered community is accounted for. Each small action of member consummation or design of strategic position will in turn affect the big things. A new unity tethered by the vision and mission now seeks expansion of membership following the same initial processes in Phase 1 and Phase 2-A.

Prior to the establishment of the Western-10 there were four members of the core group. The AT manager holds an executive middle management position in a home agency, two directors of CW agencies in counties located in the western region, and an academician from another state. The emerging AT manager constructed the vision and mission and focused on establishing high trust and value in each of the core partners. This process takes 3–12 months depending on the original disposition and type of person the manager engages with. Simultaneously, due solely on the emphasis on the mission and vision, these nucleic actors immediately assess potential allies and provide relational bridges for the manager to cross.

The AT manager continues to use a strong sense of natural curiosity to evoke change talk in each member to catalog beliefs and values that present with limitations to expansion from Phase 1 in the expansion phase. The pliability of each member and collectively yields the space to craft the strategic activities and roles engineered to effectively and efficiently impact stuck personalities and spheres. Each tethered member is valued for their strengths and is trusted to operate in them to protect the unity and equilibrium of the collaborative. In doing so, the tethered community will experience healthy growth rendering it a fit interagency operation.

Phase 3: Collaboration Diffusion/ Completion of the Expansion

Everyone in the collaboration matters. All members in the collaboration are anchored in the same understanding and operation of the mission and vision. The expansion of the group draws to completion with the Western-10 finalizing at 13 core members. Adding new members is a consensus decision of the group and the AT manager must impress upon the group the risks of getting too big. The AT manager must attend to each person relationally and as a group. Group numbers between 10 and 15 are found to be reasonable to establish and maintain trust and value in each member. The treatment for avoiding or mitigating negative impacts to the group is by the frequent feedback and communication strategies that support trust. High-quality relationships motivate and the mission holds the group accountable.

Phases 4 and 5: Collaboration, Mobilization, and Tethering Tactical Action/Family Contraction

As expansion draws to a close and each member solidifies their position and commitments to strategic plays the AT manager and tethered community move toward changing the system whether erecting an innovation, drafting policy, law, or practice changes. This movement, or wave force, can be subtle in eroding the base of an established position (such as held by a conserver) and it can topple a colossal edifice. Mobilization through AT is a tactical action. Reflection and recon assessments map the vulnerabilities obstructing the advancement of the mission and vision. Treatment via mobilization, while pointing at a specific target, will also generate a path of least resistance.

Single and plural action movements take place during mobilization and action steps. The collaboration extends and then contracts to send members out to meet with officers in various spheres of influence. The spheres of influence have no limitation since the AT operates sans hierarchy. However, there is respect and value placed in the decision of which tethered positions may interact with an officer from the governor's office or in the lower ecology of state CW leadership through health and human services. Treatments of contraction mobilization are similar to when a quarterback signals for a running back to go into motion before the ball is snapped. It is also akin to sending a delegation party to not only scout out the officers to test change readiness to adapt an innovation but takes it a step further and engages them to understand where their rationality is bonded. The conveyance and confluent activity drive the momentum of the kinetic energy of the wave. The running back in motion tests the defensive line's focus to remain in place prior to the snap of the ball. If they move, the offense moves the ball in the path of least resistance. If they remain steadfast the wave of the offense has the opportunity to tactfully utilize all players in a unified motion.

Phase 6: Core Tethering Activities/ Completion of the Contraction

Reaction from the officers and positions initially resistant to the less intrusive treatments of AT increase when a full wave of motion is released. The natural reasoning is such a treatment cannot be ignored due to the force multiplier of the unified tethered community represented. The forecasted opposition, which will manifest in an action or inaction by the targeted officers, places the AT manager in a position of peril.

The position of peril demands the AT manager to draw upon the delegated authority invested in them and operationalize it from a rapid, exacting, decision-making expertise position to avoid a power vortex. A power vortex exists when an internal or external influencer exerts force which incapacitates the collaborative efforts. Moreover, the tethered community can suffer loss of members who succumb to emotive responses derived from those thorny past experiences that vacuum formative ideas and solutions to solve key issues.

However, it can also mature as its belief system is stretched allowing ND to expose potential solutions for managing peril.

The Western-10 experienced this phase when the AT manager activated the simulation innovation at WCU. State officers from the CW section of health and human services expressed enthusiasm regarding the project and extended offers to become a partner, wanted the simulation training to spread statewide, and did not want to provide any resources to aid the project. AT engaged the state officers in various strategies to restore equilibrium to the tethered ecosystem.

Phases 7 and 8: Post-Implementation and New Management Framework/Retirement Years

The retirement years do not indicate a time for the AT manager or the AT-tethered community to kick back and relax. Instead, this post-implementation period is another phase of relational reinforcement and reflection. Norms are catalyzed and the AT manager can inculcate an operating ecology. Moreover, a natural state of tranquility is the resolve of the establishment of such norms. The new management framework facilitates a greater degree of focused work aimed at sustainability of the innovation.

In the post-implementation phase, the AT manager of the Western-10, as a natural response to such a feat, was sought by legislative officials. The recognition of the collaborative work grew statewide and beyond to other states. Officers from other jurisdictions and federal partners demonstrated interest to degrees of offering assistance and resources to aid in spreading the simulation training as well as the theory and techniques in AT management. The legislative officials tethered to the AT manager and the Western-10 to craft a new bill designed to address the deficiencies plaguing the state's for more than a decade. The AT ecology also derived a public-private hybrid between WCU and what came to be known as the REAL Academy to host the simulation training positioning it as a center of excellence and research. (Appendix A provides a flow chart representing the phased approach of AT and expected outcomes.)

All members of the Western-10 remain after four years of dedication and loyalty. The AT ecology, even during the struggles experienced with COVID-19, is steadfast in the mission. This post-implementation reflection phase furnishes the opportunity to explore decision-making and critical thinking for the next movements to address the needs of the CW staff. Decision-making, inductive and deductive reasoning and critical thinking are requisites in AT management based on the omnidirectional emphasis placed on innovation and strategies. It is the second key element in AT.

AT AND DECISION-MAKING DEVELOPMENT

Developing a relationship is a series of decisions and commitments each party enters into. The importance on developing high-quality relationships in AT directs the relational product toward elasticity to decrease negative impacts of BR and ND. Due to the high-risk/high-reward ecology of tethering the AT-tethered ecology demonstrates a command of messaging via sophisticated feedback looks driving decision points. "Advantageous decisions are made when individuals take time to learn from feedback on previous trials to adapt their decision-making strategy, developing a type of heuristic on how best to maximize profits" (Buelow & Cayton, 2020 p. 2). AT applies aspects of brain science, critical thinking, and decision-making models to foster creation of heuristics designed to maximize treatment episodes.

AT as a tethered ecology remains in motion until arriving at an equilibrium or tranquility. The factors responsible for getting from chaos to equilibrium are decision-making anchored to achieve trust, value, accountability, and motivation. The physiological, emotional, and spiritual elements of the person are directly connected to this process. As such, the negative (catabolic energy) side of decision-making can produce stress and trauma, while on the positive side (anabolic energy) elation, peace, and tranquility are produced all based on chemical reactions in the brain and body. The spiritual element falls upon the mission, which is bigger than one person or a single decision. Holistically the study and application of brain science to strengthen tethered relationships is a formidable aspect of the success of the Western-10 and AT manager. Moreover, absent a foundational understanding of brain science, investigation and exploration of decision-making would be boiled down to a mechanical process leaving public managers blind to the omnidirectional nature of humanity.

TETHERING STRANDS: TRUST, VALUE, ACCOUNTABILITY, AND MOTIVATION

Strong administrative tethering results from transparent, healthy relationships that have their resiliency tested and strengthened as the relationship deepens. To intentionally deepen the relationship, specific leadership behaviors must be present to engage, build, and maintain trust (Rock, 2010). Trust is the nucleus of the relationship—and the leaders' behavior is the process of cultivating trust.

Rock's (2010) neuroleadership model supports AT's position and findings on a scientific foundation for studying the brain's oxytocin production (anabolic energy which produces tranquility) and how leaders' behaviors can promote trust in all relationships. The basis for AT is a convergence of the innovation—toward a mutual benefit of both organizations to achieve their mission—and that cannot occur without the essential element of trust. The tethered relationship suggests that others perceive the relationship as non-threatening, solution-focused, innovative, and open through positive reinforcement. Tethering each partner by the four strands (trust, value, accountability, and motivation) positively impacts the capacity to solve complex social issues jointly, bind collaborative partners together around a common mission or goal, and generate high-quality, trusting relationships. It is only through the positive influence of the tethered relationships that micro and macro systems shift by identifying BR to change and evolve via application of ND.

QUALITY RELATIONSHIPS THROUGH ADMINISTRATIVE TETHERING LENS

As the AT manager begins to tether other managers and their organizations together to achieve organizational goals, they must ground themselves in the commonality of a singular mission, values, and purpose. This exercise gives clarity to the purpose of the quality relationship, which helps secure the AT model's purpose. Crucial to quality relationships are four critical elements, including trust, value, accountability, and motivation. Rock (2010) found eight biological factors that promote trust. The alignment of Rock's eight biological factors under AT's four developmental strands accelerates the leaders' capacity within four additional domains: decision-making and problem-solving, collaboration and influence, emotional regulation, and change agility (Rock, 2010). Ensuring both parties are highly emotionally regulated, open to change, and have similarly aligned values sets the foundation for a robust tethered connection. Through implementing systematic leadership behaviors aligned with policies and organizational philosophy, leaders create an environment where quality relationships not only thrive—but those between the leader and the workforce flourish as well (Pittman, 2019). Tethering each relationship by the four strands is a developmental exercise that requires intentionality—both initially and ongoing.

Within Zak's (2017) research, all eight of the neuroleadership behaviors link to biologically promote trust within the organization. However, through the lens of administrative tethering, some behaviors more than others lead to the promotion of trust in quality relationships within tethered relationships—both individual and with the workforce. From a holistic perspective, leaders should keep in mind that the neuroleadership behaviors align with the four developmental strands of AT.

Strand 1: Trust

Openness (Communication). Frequent, authentic, and transparent is essential for creating high trust, quality relationships that result in innovation and collaborative goals. Through candid feedback loops and dialogue, trust increases between tethered leaders and between the leader and the workforce. Both constructive and complementary communication loops are needed to build openness, trust, and vulnerability organically. Communication also reminds leaders continuously of their purpose, role, and commitment to the tethered partnership.

Natural (Vulnerability). While somewhat counterintuitive, leaders who are transparent and exhibit honesty, authenticity, and vulnerability within their tethered relationships are more apt to cultivate quality relationships, a high-trust organization, and increased workforce motivation. Leaders who interact through inquiry actively stimulate thinking, engage others, and admit to and learn from their own mistakes, amplifying the most vital leadership traits. Leaders create and attempt innovative ideas through quality relationships knowing that a growth mindset is an accepted part of the relationship. Leaders who behave in this way with their colleagues are more likely to demonstrate this behavior in their organizations with the workforce. Further, engagement with the colleague in an authentic, humble way employs the trust in the relationships as a route to improve processes, practice, and outcomes (Glisson, Green, & Williams, 2012; Janco, Salloum, Olson & Edwards, 2014; Westbrook, Ellett & Asberg, 2012). Finally, leaders who demonstrate vulnerability in partnering with others and furthering their professional development within the tethering relationship are also more likely to do so in their organizations.

Strand 2: Value

Yield (Autonomy). There is a mutual understanding within a tethered relationship of professional discernment, which gives the leader latitude to be autonomous in performing tasks independently within the context of mutual goals. Allowing each other latitude in being creative, trying new ideas, and learning from failures promotes a growth mindset within the quality relationships and, subsequently, within their organizations. Setting clear objectives that give partners in quality relationships discernment in meeting goals furthers productivity by 41 percent (Zak, 2018). Yield cultivates forward momentum within the tethered relationship.

Invest (Holistic Growth). Leaders in quality, tethered relationships have opportunities to support the balance of personal and professional commitments with each other. Leaders are in a unique position within their organizations in that they do not have peer support. Lack of peer support can sty my innovation and could negatively impact the morale of the leader. Since tethered leaders understand the isolation, stressors, and challenges associated with leading an organization, they can discuss their worries within the tethered relationship. Through supporting each other's professional development, family commitments, and professional growth opportunities, there is a magnification of trust and the relationship flourishes.

Strand 3: Accountability

Expectation (Obtainable Challenges). The ability to set both individual leaders and collaborative challenges within the tethered relationship forward momentum toward goals. Setting difficult yet attainable, time-limited challenges helps continually forward a sense of purpose about the relationship. Giving each other constructive feedback often and in real-time—including accolades—furthers trust building within the tethered relationship. As each individual within the quality relationship reaches goals, celebrating those successes spurs additional solutions to challenges and enhances trust.

Transfer (Using Strengths). One of the purposes of a tethered relationship is for each leader to use their distinct strengths, which are usually different from their colleague. Joining expertise together as a tethered team is a central purpose of the relationship. The ability to use expertise and gifts within the relationships promotes autonomy (see earlier) and increases job satisfaction, commitment, and customer service both to clients and the workforce (Zak, 2018). The tethered relationship can also serve as a learning space for both leaders, in that they have a safe place to learn, ask questions, and observe how their colleague leads.

Strand 4: Motivation

Ovation (Ccelebrating Successes). Recognizing excellent performance and celebrating the other leader's successes in public settings and with peers accelerates social equity in the relationship. When praise is specific, personal, unexpected, and spontaneous, there is oxytocin production, increasing trust dramatically (Zak, 2018). Celebrating others' meeting their goals or succeeding is core to honoring human contributions and driving the recipients to exhibit more of the same behavior. Also, as leaders recognize each other, they will begin to recognize their workforce's contributions more, cultivating a climate and culture of growth (Pittman, 2019).

Caring (Intentional Relationship). Engagement, personal knowledge about the colleague, and being "present" in interactions within the tethered collaboration invokes trust and improves the quality of the relationship. Intentionally engaging in and developing relationships with the workforce is an asset to leaders. Again, as leaders practice this with each other, they begin to do more with their workforce. A demonstration of caring within the tethered relationship not only stimulates the release of oxytocin but fosters empathy, which links to ethical behavior. Learning about leadership within the tethered relationship filters down to the leader's interactions with its workforce in multiple ways.

The AT manager's propagation of healthy brains along the way of healthy decisions establishes the ecology in tranquility. The notion of tranquility according to Simon (1947 and 1983) in a collaborative effort increases the opportunity for the fit organization subunit to apply the appropriate force to exact change in an entrenched system. Tranquility, which again approaches the physical, emotional, and spiritual person, promotes the production of oxytocin allowing positively charged anabolic energy used to stimulate critical thinking of each member in AT (Allen and Stephens, 2019). In turn, the AT manager has the ability to harness the expertise and the institution with precision to permeate the vulnerable aspects of the complex problem.

INTEGRATING A FORMALIZED CRITICAL THINKING MODEL WITH EXECUTIVE DECISION-MAKING WITHIN CPS

Senior executives face many difficult decisions and challenges, such as emerging competitors, shifts in the market resulting from new technology, and so forth. In the twenty-first century, with the advent of globalization, these challenges will continue to increase along with escalating consumer demands and expectations (Brinkholf, Gyorey, Jochim, & Norton, 2010). Often senior executives feel pressured to make decisions either to address a significant challenge or simply to appear decisive. Factors that can negatively affect executive decisions include undisciplined methodology, unfounded optimization, data overload, selective searching of evidence to support previous decisions, group thinking, lack of creditable sources, inaccurate assumptions, resistance to change, lack of vision, and bureaucratic roadblocks.

In response, multiple, sophisticated management systems and decision-support techniques have emerged (Power, 2007). These systems are divided into three primary categories: disciplined decision-making processes (e.g., formalized strategic planning), supporting management systems (e.g., total quality, balanced scorecard), and technology (e.g. executive support software, artificial intelligence systems). These systems have continued to evolve, providing senior executives with additional resources to aid in making appropriate decisions. Disciplined strategic-planning approaches can be used to aid senior executives in establishing clearly defined mission statements identifying the purpose of the organization and providing steps to help them anticipate the future direction of markets and competitors.

Total quality management and other related improvement initiatives (e.g., Six-Sigma, process reengineering) can be used to assist senior executives in accurately reviewing organizational performance and making the best decisions on how to continue to improve, reduce waste, and grow. Technology can be used by senior executives to understand organizational operations. The application of more advanced technology can even allow senior executives to simulate different scenarios and try potential solutions before implementing their ideas.

Despite the wider use of these management systems and decision-support techniques, examples of poor and failed executive decisions persist. For example, in the Challenger and Columbia shuttle disasters, information was available indicating potential problems, yet incorrect decisions were made (Porter, 2011; Shapiro, 2010). In commerce, there are multiple examples of senior executives either not being aware of a competitive threat or selecting an inappropriate response. The failure of senior executives at Blockbuster, for instance, to understand the market shift resulting from mailing DVDs rather than using video cassettes and the resulting threat from Netflix resulted in bankruptcy (Gandel, 2010). The ethical failures at a number of companies (e.g., WorldCom) and the events surrounding the recent financial meltdown are further examples of flawed executive decisions (Boerner, 2011).

In many of these situations, senior executives believed they were appropriately collecting data, checking assumptions, considering various options, and arriving at the best decisions. In hindsight, however, mistakes were made. The central question was whether there are approaches that senior executives could use to improve decisions. As an example, senior executives may be checking assumptions related to a current problem, but they may be missing an opportunity to reflect on and reconfirm the fundamental assumptions established for the organization. This step may be important when addressing a critical decision or analyzing a major shift in the marketplace.

There are options for addressing these failures, one of which has received only limited research attention: the integration of formalized critical thinking in executive decision-making processes. As noted by Harris (2007), "Critical thinking enables a leader to make decisions based on facts not on impulses, to be open minded and, most of all, acknowledging bias and prejudices and to avoid allowing them to influence decisions" (p. 12).

BACKGROUND OF THE PROBLEM

People make decisions every day, deciding what to wear, what to eat, and how to make ends meet. Senior executives in organizations are no different (Hammond, Keeny, & Raiffa, 2006), but they are also tasked with making critical decisions that affect their organizations. Often their decisions also have far-reaching effects on society (e.g., failed businesses, plant closures, loss of employees' pensions, catastrophic disasters). Deciding which course of action to take in response to a significant problem or challenge, however, is difficult and often time-sensitive. According to Elder and Paul (2004), factors that interfere with effective decisions include one-sided thinking, rushing to judgment, jumping to conclusions, failing to see issues from different points of view, working in uneven power structures, failing to notice assumptions, and using unreasonable assumptions.

Many executive decision failures led to the loss of money, opportunities, customers, or inconveniences. The problem is the scale of failures can be catastrophic in nature with loss of life, bankruptcy, and unethical behavior. Note, despite continuing improvements in supporting systems, the failures continue to occur over a long period of time from challenger to the most recent failure of blockbusters. These failures can have a devastating effect on companies, organizations, companies, and society.

Executive Decisions

The primary roles of the executive are to perform the functions of control, management, leadership, supervision, and administration (Sanders, 1999). Yet the greatest responsibility placed upon senior executives is making decisions that can have lasting effects on an organization. A person should find out what is wrong before trying to fix it (Sanders, 1999). If senior executives took this advice seriously, they might run less risk of being disappointed. Still, senior executives can run into problems along the way including underestimating uncertainty, globalization, and cross-cultural issues. Therefore, executives can deploy the most suitable approach to their decisions; apply the best models and appropriate concepts; and use relevant, accurate information and still make poor decisions.

To make effective decisions, senior executives need to build on the philosophical foundations discussed in the preceding section. Some authors have highlighted barriers that hinder executives from making effective decisions. As noted by Argyis (1994), opportunities for positive change are often wasted because senior executives fail to use critical thinking by avoiding asking necessary questions and probing for important information. Mitzberg went further, challenging senior executives to go beyond corporate myopia and raise difficult questions. According to Mintzberg (1987), the goal is to invent new facts, not rearrange old facts.

CHALLENGES TO SENIOR EXECUTIVE DECISIONS

Senior executives face difficult and complex challenges in making effective decisions. Often senior executives are faced with shifting and ill-defined goals concerning the best direction for the organization. The outcome is a high-stakes decision involving multiple stakeholders with conflicting needs and requirements. Decisions are usually made in a time-stress environment; the decision needs to be made quickly to meet the challenges of a rapidly changing environment. Finally, senior executive decisions are made against the backdrop of uncertainty. The future is not always clearly understood. The consequences of a decision are not known. The introduction of new technology or a new competitor can drastically change the landscape. Even if senior executives can address these issues, there are further challenges in the decision process.

Problems that can derail an executive decision process can include unwillingness to change (cognitive inertia), selective search for facts that support a preconceived opinion, analysis paralysis, wishful thinking, group think, underestimating uncertainty, jumping to conclusions (premature termination to seeking answers), and distortion of past experiences. Leadership, human behavior, and conflict theories are relevant to consider. These areas have greater potential for use in critical thinking.

Disciplined Decision-Making Processes

There are substantial differences between management and leadership. Managers are focused on planning, budgeting, organizing, staffing, and problem-solving. Alternatively, leaders, including senior executives, are focused on establishing strategic direction, aligning people, motivating, inspiring, and addressing pressing problems facing the organizations. To address these strategic issues, senior executives need an effective executive decision process, a disciplined approach for making difficult decisions. The goal is to achieve faster, better, and smarter decisions.

There are multiple ways to address the executive decision process including psychological, cognitive, or logical. One example in the field of economics, the rational choice theory supports the idea that individuals balance risk and rewards to make the best decisions (Chandra, Krovi, & Rajagopalan, 2008). Alternatively, potential barriers, ranging from fear of failure to the thrill of taking risks, can hinder the executive decision process.

The variety and complexity of executive decisions necessitate various phases or steps in identifying the correct option (Franklin, 2013). Welch (2001) noted that decisions should be considered as an investment: the more invested, the better chances of success. A traditional executive decision framework consists of elements and phases such as definition (identify goals), analysis (identify options), decision (chose options), reconciliation, execution, and monitor (Franklin, 2013; Mador, 2000; Murray, 2002; Krames, 2003; Welch, 2001; Wolgast, 2005). These elements and phases are reinforced by steps designed to help leaders navigate through the decision process to make the right choice, no matter the investment (Welch, 2001). In an example of nine steps to effective decision-making, Welch (2001) included the following: "Identify the objective; do a preliminary survey of options; identify the implicated values; assess the importance of the decision; budget time and energy; choose a decision-making strategy; identify options; evaluate options; and make the choice—on time, on budget" (pp. 32-44).

Another rational approach to decision analysis is Franklin's (2013) seven steps. These steps are linked to and influence each other. The decision process continues only when each step is resolved. These steps in Franklin's (2013) approach include the following: "Understanding the decision opportunity; formulate the correct goals for the decision; identify and involve the correct participants; framing the decision correctly; generate alternatives; choice— select the alternative; and learning—improve future decision-making" (p. 24). According to Franklin (2013), each part of the decision process makes a distinct role to the decision—each part controls and is controlled by each other part.

Problems can be viewed differently and from different perspectives. Accordingly, executives must solve the right problem, bring data together using documents, programs, plans, and budgets to show how the organization is functioning, and determine the best option (Sanders, 1999). Solving one problem can often create others, so executives must create an environment where solutions can be implemented (Sanders, 1999).

CRITICAL THINKING

According to Scriven and Paul (1987), critical thinking is "the intellectually disciplined process of actively and skillfully conceptualizing, applying, analyzing, synthesizing, and/or evaluating information gathered from, or generated by, observation, experience, reflection, reasoning, or communication, as a guide to belief and action" (para. 3). A further refinement of this definition is the notion of critical thinking as a "disciplined, self-directed thinking which exemplifies the perfections of thinking appropriate to a particular mode or domain of thinking" (Paul, 1990, p. 545).

CRITICAL THINKING IN BUSINESS

Although early initiatives of critical thinking were of an academic nature, the concept merged to the business community. In part, the success of an organization is dependent on the quality of thinking of its senior executives, and critical thinking is important in addressing difficult business challenges. The ability to challenge the norm is vital. Scrutinizing alternatives from a range of viewpoints to appraise the situation critically is essential to business success. In this context, critical thinking may help. In today's competitive business world, leaders must have an edge to keep their organizations competitive and successful, and that edge can be employing people who can think critically. It is not enough to hire someone with an MBA; that person needs to have critical thinking skills (Schoenberg, 2008).

According to Zori and Morrison (2009), executives "expand the concept of critical thinking by describing components that include challenging assumptions, using visualization alternatives, [considering the context of a situation], and engaging in reflective skepticism" (p. 76). Other components of critical thinking include being rational, using reflective listening, and deciding what information to trust and/or what to do next. Ennis described "the [nature] of a critical thinker that allow one to employ critical thinking skills in the course of daily life" (as cited in Zori & Morrison, 2009, p. 76).

Baldoni (2010) wrote, "Critical thinking had always been a valued attribute of leadership, but over the years, as business schools focused on quantitative and qualitative abilities, critical thinking dropped by the wayside" (para. 2). Developing critical thinking is becoming an indispensable element in academia and business. C. Roland Christensen Professor of Business Administration at Harvard Business School, David A. Garvin, told the *New York Times*, "I think there's a feeling that people need to sharpen their thinking skills, whether it's questioning assumptions, or looking at a problem from multiple points of view" (as quoted in Baldoni, 2010, para. 2). Critical thinking encourages executives to think more outside the box than with traditional thinking. According to Philley (2005),

Critical thinking encompasses deductive, inductive and lateral thinking-*Deductive thinking* looks back in time to identify and examine preceding events that were necessary and sufficient to produce the designated result-A second reasoning approach is the inductive approach through which a given fault is speculated; the investigation team then identifies and analyzes probable outcomes that result from this specific failure—*Lateral thinking* is another useful concept in incident investigation. Such thinking is popularly characterized as "thinking outside the box." When applying lateral thinking, investigators search for alternate or nontraditional explanations or solutions that fit a given set of conditions. (p. 27)

With the fast pace of the global economy, doing more with less, and cut-throat competition, senior executives must be precise and effective in their decisions. Executive decision-making is often just as fast-paced. According to Pascarella (1997), adding critical thinking to the toolbox can aid successful decision-making. In the past 20 years, the role of leadership has changed from being the person with the right answers to being the person with the right questions.

CRITICAL THINKING IN THE BUSINESS OF CHILD PROTECTION

Simon (1997) stated official networks of communications are found in every organization. Complex elements such as colloquialisms may be unique to a specific organization, region, or jurisdiction. Decision-making in an agency operates in the context of work relationships traversing vertically through the hierarchy and horizontally among peers. Simon (1997) purported decisions made by higher-ranking officials within an organization need to be communicated downward or the decisions made will have no importance. The absence of an omnidirectional communication strategy in the agency negatively impacts the culture and climate. These impacts result in irregularities and inconsistencies in decision-making which spill over into direct service.

Administrators in CW agencies utilize laws and policies designed to guide decisions. These policies and laws do not address the ever-changing landscape of complex family issues necessitating treatments maximizing elasticity of thought. The product of complex abuse and neglect cases and lack of decision discretion bolstered in critical thinking proliferate decisions of vast uncertainty on a daily basis which affect the safety of vulnerable children and the caseworkers they supervise (Benbenishty et al., 2015). Kleinig (1996) stated discretion is a fundamental and vital medium in which administrators of public agencies perform their job duties. As such, discretion is delegated by the administration to front line supervisors and line-staff based on trust. Fostering discretion via trust is required in CW based on the capricious gray areas not found in the likely clear-cut examples in policies and laws.

Critical thinking (CT) in CW agencies incorporates workplace relationships, the climate and culture of the organization, policies and laws guiding decision pathways, and delegated discretion. Rendering a decision pertaining to child safety is the result of information a caseworker has gathered regarding the child and family, and this data is filtered through personal and organizational beliefs, policy, and law. Public managers wrestle with the realities of child endangerment, providing quality services, and maintaining public trust entangled with balancing quantitative and qualitative outputs currently used in grading decision-making. Employing artificial intelligence software and quality assurance methodologies are not designed to provide abdication or replace human responsibility, which in the case of improving chaotic public service products insists on a commitment to exercising and strengthening reasoning capacity. Further elements of critical thinking include unintended consequences or adverse consequences—watch for negative results of actions taken; lateral thinking—thinking outside the box; transformational leadership—individual and open engagement (openness); and active listening—being open to all inputs or recommendations.

Senior Executive Level Critical Thinking

Senior executives are faced with increased challenges. In response, senior executives use a wide array of decision-making approaches to arrive at a key decision, as represented by the box at the top of the figure. Depending on the type of challenge being addressed, senior executives can select from an array of existing decision processes represented by the three categories: disciplined decision-making processes, supporting management systems, and technology. The idea is to add formalized critical thinking with the goal is to integrate critical thinking concepts with the executive decision-making processes to achieve enhanced and more effective decisions. If formalized critical thinking can be used at different management levels, it is also possible that critical thinking may be useful for different types of management initiatives. As an example, the formalized critical thinking model might be applicable for leaders of task forces or even cross-functional teams.

Critical thinking is used, whether formally or informally, at all levels of executive and leader decision processes within their organizations and is effective in addressing complex problems and challenges in various situations. This statement supports the idea that critical thinking works, and executives and leaders alike are encouraged to integrate it with other management initiatives (e.g., systems management, organizational development principles) to ensure the best possible answer is achieved. Training and acceptance are key factors to effective deployment. Decisions made by leaders could be more effective if critical thinking is integrated into decision-making processes. These ideas can also be beneficial to leaders at all levels of the organization who are faced with making difficult decisions. Critical thinking is being used and is effective by executives and leaders in private, government, and nonprofit organizations.

RELATIONAL DECISION-MAKING

Public managers should value those high-quality relationships as they can provide understanding of under-analyzed areas of the organization. The identification and proper mitigation of BR and ND rely upon such interconnections. The Ecology Decision-Making (EDM) model (Bauman, Dalgeish, Fluke, and Kern, 2011) provides an internal and external view of decision influences to consider as critical thinking is applied. EDM is well accepted and practiced in CW circles and is beginning to influence other academics. Fluke et al.'s model lists case factors, organizational factors, external factors, and decision-maker factors as potential influences considered for decision-making. Elements are rendered into a decision and the produced outcome should be used to examine future decisions. Case factors can include items such as statements, observations, or case history the CW worker collects in interviews and record searches. Organizational factors included any policies created to *fill in* gaps in a state policy or law. External factors such as local stakeholder, local politics, or support service limitations in the decision process. Decision-maker factors include personal and professional beliefs and bias relating to the decision subject matter. Outcomes are used to validate appropriate safe decisions and assist to correct *less-safe* decisions.

Relation-centered decision-making zooms in on a decision dyad, which can be a frontline worker and supervisor, or in the AT context, the AT manager and a tethered partner. The decision influences pass through the spectrums of BR found in each person. In order to effectively mitigate elements negatively impacting one's decision pathway, another person with an ability to recognize the bounded belief must be incorporated. A high-quality, tethered relationship facilitates a resilient ability to challenge areas where one's rationality is bound. Vulnerabilities in trust must be tempered carefully. When distrust is detected in oneself or in another it should be explored. These vulnerabilities, if left unattended, will result in intractable and diminished relationship. When immediately attended to it will generate stronger trust.

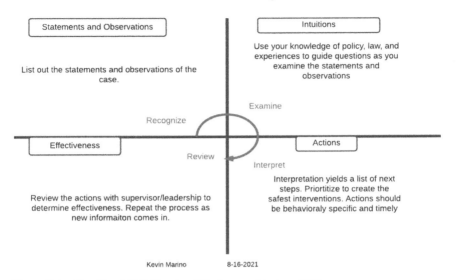

Figure 5.1   The Good Call Quadrant™. *Source:* Marino, 2021.

Relational elasticity pronounced by ND is the space in which BR is treated and decision-making matures. The maturation of the decision process explored in either a dyadic expression as illustrated in the figure, or manifests in a polyadic ecology as found in AT. The iterative process of consistent commitment to critically think through areas of BR via the lens of the group's mission and application of palliative treatment of ND to individuals and members of the interagency arrangement carries through the life cycle of tethered network.

For example, the AT manager believed working with elected officials would generate energy required to urge state partners to supply resources for the simulation project. The AT manager and several others believed it was premature. Two decision options were on the table. The first is to move forward with the garnered support of the few and engage with elected officials. The second is to listen and reflect on what the majority of the tethered community is advising. Application of critical thinking provides the AT manager and the tethered community ability to examine all the facts, reflect, examine assumptions (BR) and respond effectively to ND. The result of this application was a crafted plan to once again participate in negotiations with state partners and draw hard lines signaling permission to the AT manager and Western-10 delegates to call in elected officials.

Magnification of the BR and ND Dyad:
The Good Call Quadrant™

At each decision point and relational stage, a four-quadrant diagram was constructed by the AT manager to apply decision-tracing methodology as depicted in figure 5.1. This treatment was specifically designed to operationalize the key aspects in the critical decision model and reflective process characterized in AT. It deconstructs and traces the decision-making process, which gives way to multiple decisional and actionable paths. Recognizing the facts surrounding the decision facilitates questions to explore through examination of such facts. As a set of facts are interpreted discovery of BR is clarified through the lens of the mission. Focused strategic operations can then be designed and deployed. Lessons of importance are cataloged as well as any items requiring research to inform the critical thinking process.

The Good Call Tool was derived from forensic applications I used in profiling criminal cases. Douglas (1999, 2006) uses a four-quadrant method, which inspired the Good Call Tool, to list case information, apply decision process models, assess the crime, and profile a perpetrator. The Good Call Tool is a four-quadrant system that relies on an iterative process using the cycle of recognition, examination, interpreting, and reviewing information. Recognition of statements and observations relevant to a case is the first application. Most of the time CPS caseworkers have too much information and their challenge is sorting to find the relevant pieces and recycling what is not needed. To maintain objectivity, it requires the CPS professional to have a high-quality relationship with CPS law and policy, which define what a legal fact is. The intuition quadrant is the first stage of filtering information as it is examined through the lens of CPS law and policy. This is how BR can be identified and mitigated with ND. Actions are then formulated as the intuition is interpreted through CPS law and policy. Finally, reviewing the effectiveness of an action or set of actions with the supervisor or leadership maintains the safest interventions are applied in a CPS case. As new information comes in the cycle starts all over considering previous information. This tool and process is highly effective with CPS frontline professionals. As such, it was applied in the AT decision schema.

As the Western-10 formed, this quadrant was created to assist with tracing decision-making. The information driving the argument for change as cited in chapter 2 would all fall in the upper left quadrant. The management and catalog of relevant information is necessary to avoid focus drift. The purpose for the change is to improve education, training, and decrease secondary stress for CW staff, which is also a fact. The upper right quadrant is to list questions related to the mission and to each member. The AT manager asks questions pertaining to trust, value, and belief to formulate emerging areas of BR. ND is then negotiated in the lower right quadrant as new actions emerge and finally moves toward the lower left quadrant for review and reflection of the limitations found at the individual and group levels. The process is cyclical in nature and the AT manager reengages when new information emerges.

The Good Call Quadrant has multiple applications utilized throughout the AT process. It was used in direct practice in the simulation training to assist frontline staff in developing stronger critical thinking methods as they assessed maltreatment. In direct practice, this method improved decisions through listing facts of the case, policy, and law. It fostered frontline staffs' ability to self-identify and accept feedback from the trainers regarding BR, which in turn facilitates mailable ND.

HOW CRITICAL THINKING IS APPLIED THROUGH THESE MODELS

The three models discussed previously each act as a focusing lens. The EDM is the larger lens, the BR and ND dyad is a smaller lens magnifying the specific decision-maker and the person assisting to make this decision. Finally, the Good Call Quadrant is yet a smaller lens greatly magnifying the smaller elements found in the decision process. A three-lens view captures those elements typically studied separately, and rarely considered corporately (Fluke, et al., 2020). The public manager can move in an out of each layer focusing on a specific decision space or the entire plain. Moreover, it contains the proven characteristics and processes listed in the current critical thinking literature. Decisions in the public services arena are conducted *per necessitudinem*. Decisions are for, about, with, and through relationships. Critical thinking applications in AT are to inculcate the value of the person in which the decision is for or about. In doing so, decision-making remains focused on a framework of relational trust centered on a mission.

SUMMARY: CONTRIBUTION TO THE FIELD

We have all been there, in a hurried early morning environment; we try to render a decision with very little time to think and to take action that is deemed appropriate. We close our eyes, take a breath and hope that at the end of the night everyone will enjoy the dinner. Importantly, you learn that the key spice ingredient chosen earlier in the day made the meal. And whimsically you recall that morning many years ago when your grandmother taught you the rule-of-thumb to remember when you need to select a suitable spice for a main course a broccoli and spinach lasagna when served in the middle of winter.

This vignette illustrates an important facet of how people, like the public administrator or the local chef, render decisions on behalf of others. Amid a high level of uncertainty and chaos people satisfice, they consult their experiences and with a measure of confidence they act. But what if their perception is not precise and their learnt assumptions related to the situation are misapplied? The wrong decision is made thus resulting in difficulties for others. Simon (p.118) provides seminal guidance to this worry when he notes in *Administrative Behavior* (1997) that the

> central concern of Administrative theory is peculiarly the theory of intended and bounded rationality—of the behavior of human beings who satisfice because they have not the wits to maximize. . . . Limited rationality was defined largely as a residual category a departure from rationality and the positive characterization of the process of choice was very incomplete.

From Simon's notion we see that people, for the most part, cannot figure it all out; they need to rely upon what they have learnt and experienced and apply it for better or for worse. Second, although this human challenge is pervasive, Simon seems to hint of an opportunity to enhance the scope of such decision-making. This opportunity may manifest in cognitive devices such as those involving heuristics, intuition, or rules-of-thumb. The story does not necessarily end here. Let's turn now to AT and how it couples with these devices.

Simon relates that the exercise of intuition with those individuals with expert knowledge. Such experts typically have 50,000 pieces of data at their cognitive avail surrounding a subject area. This cognitive capacity allows them to render decisions quickly and effectively; they can think and act with a likely positive outcome. However, this capacity is a finite, limited resource for the organization. Most organizations do not have such a cognitive capacity at their (constant) behest. Organizations that provide for the CPS social product exemplify such a type of an (public/private/nonprofit) organization. This, then, is where AT lends value. AT, through its intervening capacity (i.e., its work with the Western-10), orchestrates sub-areas of limited expertise; these sentinels of expertise, as it is safely assumed, lack the 50,000 pieces of data to qualify as experts as Simon (1997) prescribes. But collectively they may.

Enter the AT manager. The AT manager then strategically aligns these areas of limited expertise sufficient to yield collective expert action necessary for the positive disposition of the social product (i.e., the needed CPS service). AT thus distills the decision-choice-action apparatus, as exercised amid rationality that is bounded, and imbues it with greater cognitive precision to extend its decision-making capacity. In this sense and importantly, AT fosters a useful contingency when the limitations of satisficing become real. The realities that materialize either tend to lead to difficulties for the individual, or, in the unfortunate extreme, manifest in the complex public problem that results in tragedy for the innocent. AT, as discerned from the vantage of the decision-choice-action apparatus, is the essence of our small attempt to apply our interpretation of Simon's colossal scholarly legacy in a useful manner.

Chapter 6

Conclusion

The inspiration for this book retains a focus upon those challenges and barriers intrinsic to the effective, meaningful, and sustained implementation of collaboration as necessitated by a complex public problem and/or public imperative. Wright (2009) focused on initial research that examined federal programming as implemented through a federal, state, and local collaborative arrangement. This research, along with ensuing work, maintained a focus upon the area involving the effectiveness of public sector collaboration from its inception to its workplace application. The literature reviewed surrounding such collaboration identified two schools of thought. One perspective argues the overriding, central import of the hierarchy to the area of public sector collaboration as versus the second, sans (without) hierarchical perspective that embraces the notion that those "liked-mined" actors who engage in collaboration are the prime influencers surrounding its conduct. These vantages prompted further consideration related to how they could be conceptually fused to enrich understanding as to the effective design of a collaboration. The approach comports to the multifaceted challenges faced by today's public managers who are summoned to address a complex problem through a collaborative framework.

Wright and Shiner (2017) accordingly developed the Shiner-Wright Collaboration Model (SWM); their archetype construed an approach to collaboration that considers both the hierarchical and the sans hierarchy schools of thought. The SWM identifies a milieu in which the various oversight, frontline service, and command structural components exist in a churn mechanism as conducted in a dynamic, operating ecology through a set of venues. Wright and Shiner (2017) submitted this approach to shed further insights concerning the core tasks and functions germane to the conduct of collaboration. A key facet of such an analytical lens involved the introduction and application of Administrative Tethering (AT) framework (Wright, 2009; Shiner-Wright, 2017). AT manifests through a series of interagency bonding actions and techniques to address the multidimensional nature of a complex, pressing public problem. Collaborative partners are brought together via transcending, multi-messaging modalities; this intervention aims to inculcate high levels of trust, value, accountability, and motivation at the partnering level. Simon notes that this AT goal must be balanced against its implementation costs (1962, 2001, 2002).

The Marino-Wright Model (MWM) ascribes and depicts further dimensions of the AT function; its functional areas consider an operational ecology in which equilibration of power is a prime objective of the AT manager. This condition can then help the public manager (and others) secure and preserve the (sustained) delivery of a needed social product to the public. Nonetheless, to render the MWM meaningful, it necessitated further research to address the actual set of challenges intrinsic to the delivery of a public service (i.e., CPS). Such an imperative is reinforced by Simon's caution that the researcher needs to carefully examine how one's theory manifest in the reality of the practice (Simon, 1948, 1957, 1976, 1977, 1998, 2013). Simon further emphasizes that this approach will help the researcher to contemplate the actual behavior of the individual more effectively; such cognition can then enable a more complete research design to uncover the essence of a phenomenon (Simon, 2002). The development of such a knowledge path related to AT embraced a practitioner-scholar dynamic as guided by three goals:

a) Bridge the gap between the practitioner's deep knowledge and experiences of a specific complex public service provider and the academic research;
b) Classify the facts in colloquial and academic terms and frameworks to improve accuracy; and
c) Allow the powerful description, utility for other managers to replicate it, and predict outcomes with greater clarity.

These goals, along with Simon's behavioral perspectives, were deeply ensconced in the eventual development work that was undertaken and involved the Western-10 collaboration. This entity emerged as central as AT was explored through the classical practitioner-academic orientation. This review provided insights as to how Simon's perspectives of bounded rationality (BR) and near decomposability (ND) mediated with AT. The mediation of AT with the notions of ND and BR fashioned a conceptual model that was soon applied as a diagnostic tool to aid in the more involved phases of the Western-10 development work. The AT, as an intervention, was applied to an extant CPS operating ecology that was eventually shaped over a seven-year period. The fruit of this work yielded a training innovation that was rendered operational with overwhelming, ongoing positive feedback as measured and analyzed. The AT manager fundamentally assessed how this training innovation was diffused throughout the collective and local ecologies of those member counties of the Western-10 collaboration. This assessment involved a careful examination as to the notions of AT-BR-ND that may have induced this diffusion.

The aim of this analytical foray was to better understand how local ecological precursors formed a transit that subsequently enhanced the formation of those Western-10 collaboration mechanisms employed to turn a worthy ambition that then morphed into a complex vision. As led by a seasoned manager who then applied a new, untested concept to bring cognitive order to this vision. This action garnered a measure of neutral-competent support from the practice and academic realms that, in turn, raised its own measurement bar with alignment to the scholarship made available by Professor H. A. Simon. Simon's perspectives, as applied, helped to frame and enable a unique practitioner-academic arrangement designed to implement state-of-the-art simulation training to newly hired CPS to fill entry-level positions throughout the Western-10 Collaborative. The question remains: In summary why and how did AT contribute to such a change process pertaining to the delivery of the CPS social product to those North Carolina (NC) counties comprising the Western-10 Collaborative?

To come to some sense of closure surround the nature of AT here, and, in turn to unite the implications arising from this query compels further examination as to the nature of the AT Ecosystem Mediation process. Such an analytical orientation involves the review of two of Simon's ND claims (Simon, 2002):

1. At any level of complexity, nearly decomposable systems will evolve much faster than systems of comparable complexity that are not nearly decomposable; and
2. Thus, this second claim, unlike the first one, does not predict a steady increase in the complexity of the systems that are evolving; what it predicts is a growing predominance, at all levels of complexity, of systems that are nearly decomposable. (p. 592)

Importantly, these claims then need to be further construed in terms of Simon's characterization as to the broader, conceptual contours of the ND (Simon, 2002):

The Model of a nearly decomposable arrangement consists of a federation of multi-level subsystems. The property of ND features a special characteristic is that equilibrating capacity involving interactions within subsets at any level take place much more rapidly than the interactions between subsystems at that same level, and similarly all the way to upper levels of its hierarchical structure. ND systems have very special dynamic behavior when disturbed from equilibrium. In turn, the subsets at the lowest of the system return to equilibrium while the sets at the next level above are still changing dynamically (relatively slowly), and similarly (and even more decisively) for the still higher levels, which are essentially stationary on this time scale. (p. 589)

AT, when considered through the framework of ND, provides a unique, critical differentiator when gauging the fitness of an interagency, collaborative entity designated to mitigate a complex public problem. If the collaboration participants are construed as ND "subunits," then conceptually, AT may exercise its capacity to strategically intervene among the hierarchical levels to catalyze actions that help to materialize a more effective and efficient ND response system.

Importantly, the AT intervention, as enabled through the interagency entity, can apply adjustments as to BR and/or ND in order to render "fitness" to this collectivity. Simon directs attention to the accruing benefits to such AT actions by noting that is not that more complex systems will evolve more rapidly than less complex systems but that, at any level of complexity, nearly decomposable systems will evolve much faster than systems of comparable complexity that are not ND. Thus, this "second claim, unlike the first one, does not predict a steady increase in the complexity of the systems that are evolving; what it predicts is a growing predominance, at all levels of complexity, of systems that are nearly decomposable" (Simon, 2002, p. 592).

The fitness of this ND response system can continue to mitigate the complex problem as encountered if, and only if, the interagency subunit members meet the demands imposed by the prescriptions resulting from the AT-BR-ND mediation process. The Leadership held responsible for the performance of their staff in this newly constituted interagency response arrangement must ensure that their ongoing work comports with the rigor ascribed to these prescriptions as based upon staff familiarity with the local grindstone.

ND MAINTENANCE AND SUSTAINABILITY CYCLE

The (condition of the) local grindstone, much like a lighthouse, functions as an important sentinel of information for the AT manager to consult to estimate the likelihood that the current fit condition of the interagency entity will be maintained. Simon provides that in the long term, the complex problem can continue to be allayed by this entity due to its level of fitness.

The overarching question that then needs to be posed is, if it is given that AT was directly responsible for sustainability of the Western-10 sustainability (without any additional state resources) then how was such a feat accomplished?

The lighthouse has provided vital situational awareness information to the professional mariner since its inception many, many years ago. During the 1800s, for instance, the world trade emanating from Salem, Massachusetts, depended upon the lighthouse to assist those vessels who needed access to its ports. The lighthouse has saved many lives due to its ability to deliver appropriate information to the right person, in the right fashion, and at the right time. The utility of such a set of such detail is meant to mitigate a complex problem in a manner that cojoined many individuals as orchestrated by a seasoned captain of the sea.

The need for this device cannot be underestimated and the accompanying implications it conjures cannot be ignored. Upon reflection, one is compelled to consider the concept of precision. Precision in such a context is underwritten by expertise and trust. These two areas tend not to manifest in a perfunctory fashion. Rather, they can materialize if not taken for granted by those who lead. The hope here is that the executive-level public leader, enmeshed in the cacophony of accoutrements that accompany the hurried world of officialdom, may, during a moment of tranquility, ponder the utility of the lighthouse and perhaps consider its historical capacity to facilitate the safe conduct of a collaborative involving international commerce. But to extend this reach beyond a glance is unlikely for a variety of reasons; the reasons for such limited outreach have been exhaustively thought thru by public administrative scholars such as Downs, Weber, Golembiewski, Waldo, Kettl, and so on.

For those who wish to partake in learning as to the complex realities that govern the practice involving an interagency orientation as initiated by the complex problem will be exposed (or should) to unfamiliar areas of expertise. This encounter will be exhausting. In the long term, this effort will generate a wealth of knowledge concerning the power of expertise as well as the power of trust. Trust and expertise underwrite much of what is done in life ranging from the common to the infrequent. To operate both areas in tandem requires precision; precision can be cursorily casted as a "science and craft." But this descriptive produces a direction of thought, but this is not enough. To generate the proper dose of critical thinking upon this subject matter calls for a highly sophisticated understanding of the notion of precision. Such an understanding is only realized with the proper level of understanding, via an unwavering intellectual devotion, as to how trust and expertise mediate and cojoin. Enjoyment must accompany the long-haul nature of such personal enrichment.

For purposes here, acquisition of such insights can then be juxtaposed and applied to those public matters requiring an interagency sequestering to rid the public of a looming threat. Those leaders who come to such a moment must impress upon other like-minded leaders of equal rank the mitigation power of trust and expertise as it relates to this public threat. This transformed leader can then exhibit a stronger step when approaching those who exercise their well-earned expertise in the interagency response setting and whose trust has been earned and cemented. This type of leader can then meaningfully contribute to such vital response if expressed and delivered at an appropriate distance.

AT and its impact upon the conduct of the interagency collaboration harkens a return to the lighthouse. The AT manager could gain some important insights from the sea captain who relied heavily upon the information provided by the lighthouse to safely conduct a type of commerce as it existed over 200 years ago. Sharing a cup of fish chowder drawn from the same kettle, the captain and the AT manager would probably discuss the nature of their experiences in the field as encountered while tethered to their respective home agencies or dock from which their assignments commenced. Certainly, after sharing the numerous insights gained from responding to the numerous needs of the public bureau, the AT manager could relate that the heart of the AT function can be distilled down to the notions of trust and expertise. The AT manager would then explain AT centers upon the availability of trustworthy relationships as well as the effective application of diverse areas of expertise given the complexities of the extant public problem. Collectively, these imperatives pose significant demands upon the AT manager. In an effort to reconcile the scope of such demands and their accompanying performance requirements draws attention to a set of influential theoretical frameworks as construed by Simon (1962, 2001, 2002).

ND INTERAGENCY FITNESS DEVELOPMENT AND MAINTENANCE CYCLE

The AT manager must make sense of a massive amount of information, data, and assumptions accorded with an area of expertise. The AT manager must also consider that these experts could render opinions that are partly based upon misplaced perceptions. These reflections inspired a focus upon Simon's perspectives of BR and ND. These frameworks were applied to more effectively understand the impact of AT as manifested in the work of the AT manager in relation to the Western-10 Collaborative. The totality of this analysis was reviewed and depicted in various incarnations. These analytical items point toward the need to ascribe a cycle concerning the conduct of AT as identified and detailed as follows:

Part 1. 1. AT Manager trust instilled 2. support institution sponsored protocol 3. credibility established 4. BR improved/changes / 5. ND improved fit organization 6. mitigate complex problem 7. Interagency now predominates 8. AT manager equilibrates 9. preserves regular delivery of social product 10. Institutional Expertise/Expert assume new role of AT manager of the Venues 1-3 and fosters new alignment of collective expert practice

Part 2. 11. Expert Manager trust instilled 12. support institution sponsored protocol 13. credibility established 14. BR improved/changes / 15. ND improved/adjusted fit organization 16. mitigate complex problem 17. Interagency continues to predominate 18. Institutional Expert (as new AT manager) equilibrates 19. preserves regular delivery of social product 20. Maintenance Cycle repeats 11-20.

When examining this cycle, the key milestones are reflected in 1–20 with 1–10 reflecting Part 1 and 11–20 reflecting Part 2. Upon completion of Part 2, milestones 11–20 repeats itself. This cycle helps to maintain the ND fitness at the service level due to its monitoring capacity. The notion of trust, as reflected in high-quality interpersonal bonds, is highly salient in terms of addressing the implications associated with BR as based upon the given context of the interagency collaborative. From another vantage, the individual may have a misplaced perspective pertaining to his/her role within the organization. This negative perception calls for remediation that, in turn, would draw upon the skills of the AT manager. These sets of AT interactions foster a mediation process involving the framework of AT-BR-ND; the key facets of this process are highlighted here.

The key, interesting residue from the AT intervention is that by instilling trust within the operating ecology of the collaboration, its stakeholders (as subunits) can arrive at deeper, meaningful cognition as to how their respective capacitates align with the other participants of the interagency response entity. Through a careful design, the AT manager can merge these distinct areas of expertise that then can foster a guiding ND maintenance protocol that is anchored in and united upon these unique areas of expert intrinsic to the interagency collaborative. This re-tooled entity then can be led by an expert manager properly equipped to conduct the ensuing maintenance schedule as depicted in Part 2 discussed earlier.

The work with the Western-10 Collaborative rendered key insights in terms of the utility and relevance of AT as a fresh conceptual construct to approach the area of the interagency collaboration. This work identified several important implications:

1. In relation to Simon's notion of ND, *AT has the capacity to intervene in a directed fashion such that it can help hasten an organizational,*

hierarchical response to a power disequilibrium involving its service delivery system. The AT manager can strategically guide this adjustment and equilibrate such a power imbalance.

2. The AT manager, with a system can then deem the interagency collaboration as fit, and with such fitness it then can predominate over the complex problem and rid the society of a pressing public threat and maintain the delivery of the social product to the public.

3. As based upon findings from both qualitative and quantitative research and analysis, the perspectives of AR-ND-BR have a collective impact when engaged in a purposive mediation process.

4. The ND conceptual framework applies to the work undertaken by the Western-10 Collaborative. This notion aligns with and gains support when Simon highlights that ND "provides a very basic property is shared by almost all complex systems observed in nature (inorganic as well as organic, stretching from elementary particles to social systems)."

Collectively, these implications are relevant to the nature of the contributions and outcomes of the work of the Western-10 Collaborative; this posit is reinforced in terms of the expert-driven training innovation that it produced. The AT-BR-ND mediation process fostered a highly precise developed system that eventually rendered a robust training system that emerged from an excessively turbulent ecology unscathed. This outcome has generated a reservoir of confidence and goodwill to help realize and diffuse other such innovative offerings designed to benefit the CPS practice realm concerning those NC counties involved in the Western-10 Collaborative

AT IN THE CONTEXT OF RELATIONSHIP, TRUST, AND DECISION-MAKING

Public service members' and administrators' functionality orbit in the atmosphere of relationship. Attempts to swing the pendulum of efficiency too far by thinning the bonds between the service recipient-provider and the service provider-administrator threaten service quality. Professionals that join the public service membership most often do so from a desire to help others. AT teaches us a loss of perspective of the responsibility we hold to invest in our organizational members will indeed result in lowered precepting of value and trust.

If trust is the nucleus of a relationship, then value is the nutrient that fosters mature growth. Each member is then tethered to the mission to serve individuals and families in crisis. The strength of the relational bond is dependent on the resources allocated to nurture the members attached. An unfit organization gain receives the palliative treatment rendered through AT and sets the pathway for recovery.

High-quality relationships cultivated through the process outlined in family life cycle (FLC) learn to exercise a greater rate of effective decision-making due to their ability to identify BR generating elasticity for innovation through ND. Public managers may then begin to address larger systemic issues outside the home agency and expand the tethered ecology much as described in the Western-10 example. The three cascading processes of relationship building, brain science, and critical thinking were intentionally adopted to address the whole person as the challenges with collaboration were considered.

FINAL THOUGHTS

What is to be learned from our review of the notion of AT? To properly address the essence of this query prompts a return to the discussion surrounding the lighthouse. Specifically, we rejoin the captain and the AT manager as they review the finer points of their respective experiences negating the complex web of human-human interactions that help them to approximate a modular path to resolve their respective problems. Interestingly, although their relationship-building work called for much time and attention to detail what remained was a legacy of learning as secured in the attributes of trust and expertise.

When we think of the lighthouse and its capacities to save lives, we must consider its unique ability to unleash a broad swath of light upon rough seas. This welcomed illumination aids the captain to navigate the perils of such weather sea and attain safe harbor for the ship and its crew. The ability of the captain to surmount such dangers hinges upon the degree of trust that the ship crew places in his professional skills and expertise as a shipmaster. The ability to carry out such a feat requires the captain to strategically orchestrate the work of the crew such that they respond in earnest to the captain's well-timed, informed directives. Trust at this level sources the captain's credibility that then promotes a valuable reservoir of goodwill; the benefits of this additive materializes when the individual members of the ship's crew disregard the needs of the self and enjoin the ship's higher calling as defined the set of traditions, mores, norms, and culture of their chosen profession.

It is essential that the captain continues to devote time and energy in the maintenance of such high-quality crew relationships. The captain will rely upon such well-honed rapports in times when the seas become ferocious. It is as such moments of intense chaos the strength of the relationships serves their vital function. These strong bonds enable the captain to engage the various subunits of the ship's crew to function together as a team to provide the needed assistance to the captain as the vital information provided by the lighthouse is optimized. This interunit adaptation then helps the captain to blaze a path that then can draw such a complex traverse to a close as all are now instilled in the "tranquility" of a safe harbor. Such a safe traverse serves as a mark of a fit organization as embodied by the ship's crew and as led by their captain.

Like the captain, the AT manager applies precision to efforts devoted to developing rapports with those individuals deemed central to the successful development of the Western-10 Collaborative. The AT manager engaged this development work by exhaustively considering the internal as well as external impacts of these persons upon the Western-10 Collaborative as understood through the mediation of the AT-BR-ND perspectives. The AT manager then leveraged the power of these two perspectives to fashion a conceptual "Intervention Landscape." This conceptual construct served as the area in which the AT manager channeled such high-quality relationships. As positioned, these relationships then helped the AT manager to reinforce the capacity of the Western-10 Collaborative to respond to and evolve given the numerous complex challenges encountered.

What was learned from our experience working with the practitioners and scholars devoted to the development of the Western-10 Collaborative is that indeed public administration theory is not fragmented in nature; the findings related to the mediation of AT with Simon's perspectives of BR and ND highlights this thought. Like many, we also experienced the joy of working with Simon's profound scholarship. This encounter exposed us to the notion of "Simon Time." Indeed, such reads required a reservation of 3–4 blocks of time to properly engage our cognitive development path as consumers of such dense literature. With these nuggets of accumulated knowledge in hand, a set of key implications arose with impacts related to the short-term, the long term, and the still longer term.

AT taught us an important lesson regarding the classical practice-theory interchange. Simon's wisdom lent us welcomed prescriptions here. He has repeatedly cautioned that scholarly attention must remain steadfast in its effort for theory to be construed as relevant to the practice. However, the "how to" of such a task calls for a steady flow of critical thinking. We then focused our attention upon how public administration theories can circulate within a milieu that is familiar to a cadre of practitioners. For us, Simon's prescription regarding the utility of theory was taken to heart. Out of necessity, we maintained a steady presence at the AT helm for the CPS practice to value the utility of public administration diagnostics on a lasting basis.

In conclusion, our tour with AT impressed upon us that the public administration field should reconsider the scholar-practitioner interchange as it concerns its capacity to inform those interagency entities that materialize to address (and readdress) a complex problem that impinges upon the public. Such an interagency construct prompted us to consider a practitioner-theory-practitioner orientation as a more effective construct to attain applied knowledge that more properly approximates the urgent needs of the practice. This construct proved exceedingly useful aiding the Western-10 Collaborative in its journey to acquire the safe harbor that is now regarded as its own.

Bibliography

Alabi, K. (2020). A 2020 perspective on "Digital blockchain networks appear to be following Metcalfe's law". *Electronic Commerce Research and Applications, 40*, 100939. doi: 10.1016/j.elerap.2020.100939

Allen, E., Lyons, H., & Stephens, J. C. (2019). Women's leadership in renewable transformation, energy justice and energy democracy: Redistributing power. *Energy Research & Social Science, 57*, 1–11 doi: 10.1016/j.erss.2019.101233

Amoako-Gyampah, K., Meredith, J., & Loyd, K. W. (2018). Using a social capital lens to identify the mechanisms of top management commitment: A case study of a technology project. *Project Management Journal, 49*(1), 79–95. doi:10.1177/875697281804900106

Amsler, L. (2016). Collaborative governance: Integrating management, politics, and law. *Public Administration Review, 76*(5), 700–711. doi: 10.1111/puar.12605

Andersson, R., Eriksson, H., & Torstensson, H. (2006). Similarities and differences between TQM, six sigma and lean. *TQM Magazine, 18*(3), 282.

Andrew, S., Short, J. Kyujin J., & Arlikatti, S. (2015). Intergovernmental cooperation in the provision of public safety: Monitoring mechanisms embedded in interlocal agreements. *Public Administration Review, 75*(3), 401–410. doi: 10.1111/puar.12312

Ansell, C., & Gash, A. (2008). Collaborative governance in theory and practice. *Journal of Public Administration Research and Theory, 18*(4), 543–571. doi:10.1093/jopart/mum032

Armat, M. R., Assarroudi, A., Rad, M., Sharifi, H., & Heydari, A. (2018). Inductive and deductive: Ambiguous labels in qualitative content analysis. *The Qualitative Report, 23*(1), 219–221.

Arnold, J. A., Arad, S., Rhoades, J. A., & Drasgow, F. (2000). The empowering leadership questionnaire: The construction and validation of a new scale for measuring leader behaviors. *Journal of Organizational Behavior, 21*(3), 249–269.

Armat, M. R., Assarroudi, A., Rad, M., Sharifi, H., & Heydari, A. (2018). Inductive and deductive: Ambiguous labels in qualitative content analysis. *The Qualitative Report, 23*(1), 219–221.

Avoyan, E., Tatenhove, J., & Toonen, H. (2017). The performance of the Black Sea Commission as a collaborative governance regime. *Marine Policy, 81*, 285–292. doi: 10.1016/j.marpol.2017.04.006

Baldoni, J. (2010). How leaders should think critically. *Harvard Business Review Blog.* Retrieved July 27, 2012, from http://blogs.hbr.org/baldoni/2010/01/how _leaders_should_think_criti.html

Bartholet, E. (2015). Differential Response: a dangerous experiment in child welfare. *Florida State University Law Review, 3*, 573.

Bass, B. (1985). *Leadership and performance, beyond expectations.* New York: The Free Press.

Berardo, R. & Lubell, M. (2016). Understanding what shapes, a polycentric governance system. *Public Administration Review, 76*(5,) 738–751. doi: 10.1111/puar.12532

Berlanda, S., Pedrazza, M., Trifiletti, E., & Fraizzoli, M. (2017). Dissatisfaction in child welfare and its role in predicting self-efficacy and satisfaction at work: A mixed-method research. *BioMed Research International, 2017*, 5249619. doi: 10.1155/2017/5249619

Bland, J. M., & Altman, D. G. (1996). Measurement error and correlation coefficients. *BMJ: British Medical Journal, 313*(7048), 41–42.

Boerner, H. (2011). First decade of the 21st century and corporate governance: Success or failure: Which marked the 2000–2010 period? *Corporate Finance Review, 15*(6), 31–35.

Borovic, F., Cingula, D., & Primorac, D. (2013, April 5). Information system support for decision making in public administration. In D. Filipovic & A. G. Urnaut (Eds.), *Economic and social development: Book of proceedings of the 2nd International Scientific Conference* (pp. 922–930). Retrieved from https://publications.hse.ru/en /books/97218162

Bozeman, B., & Johnson, J. (2015). The political economy of public values: A case for the public sphere and progressive opportunity. *The American Review of Public Administration, 45*, 61–85. doi: 10.1177/0275074014532826

Brinkholf, A., Gyorey, T., Jochim, M., & Norton, S. (2010). *The challenges ahead for supply chains: McKinsey Global Survey Results.* New York: McKinsey & Company

Brookhart, S. M. (2018). Learning is the primary source of coherence in assessment. *Educational Measurement, Issues and Practice, 37*(1), 35–38.

Bryer, T. (2009). Explaining responsiveness in collaboration: administrator and citizen role perceptions. *Public Administration Review, 69*(2), 271–283. doi: 10.1111/j.1540-6210.2008.01973.x

Bryson, John M. (07/01/2014). Public value governance: Moving beyond traditional public administration and the new public management. *Public Administration Review* (0033–3352), *74*(4), 445.

Buelow, M. T., & Cayton, C. (2020). Relationships between the big five personality characteristics and performance on behavioral decision making tasks. *Personality and Individual Differences, 160*, 1-11 doi: 10.1016/j.paid.2020.109931

Chandler, S. M. (2017). Managing innovative collaborations: The role of facilitation and other strategies for working collaboratively. *Human Service Organizations: Management, Leadership, and Governance, 41*, 133–146. doi: 10.1080/23303131.2016.1229708

Chandra, A., Krovi, R., & Rajagopalan, B. (2008). Risk visualization: A mechanism for supporting unstructured decision-making processes. *International Journal of Applied Management and Technology 6*(4), 48–70.

Child Protective Services Intake Lacks Consistency (2019). https://www.ncleg.gov/PED/Reports/documents/CPS/CPS_Report.pdf

Chiu, Y.-L., & Cross, T. P. (2020). How a training team delivers simulation training of child protection investigators. *Children & Youth Services Review, 118*, N.PAG. doi: 10.1016/j.childyouth.2020.105390

Christensen, D. (2016). Conciliation, uniqueness and rational Toxicity1. *Noûs* (Bloomington, Indiana), *50*(3), 584–603.

Conner, T. (2015). Collaboration: Exploring the role of shared identity in the collaborative process. *Public Administration Review, 76*(2), 288–301. doi: 10.1111/puar.1241

Courvoisier, D. S., Nussbeck, F. W., Eid, M., Geiser, C., & Cole, D. A. (2008). Analyzing the convergent and discriminant validity of states and traits: Development and applications of multimethod latent state-trait models. *Psychological Assessment, 20*(3), 270–280.

Cowan, G., & Arsenault, A. (2008). Moving from monologue to dialogue to collaboration: The three layers of public diplomacy. *The ANNALS of the American Academy of Political and Social Science, 616*(1), 10–30. doi: 10.1177/0002716207311863

Creswell, J. W. (2013). *Qualitative inquiry & research design: Choosing among five approaches* (3rd ed.). Thousand Oaks, CA: Sage.

Cushman, D. (2008). Reed's law and how multiple identities make the long tail just that little bit longer. In *Recent trends and developments in social software* (pp. 123–130). Berlin, Heidelberg: Springer.

Cyrus, J. W., Santen, S. A., Merritt, C., Munzer, B. W., Peterson, W. J., Shockley, J., & Love, J. N. (2020). A social network analysis of the western journal of emergency medicine special issue in educational research and practice. *The Western Journal of Emergency Medicine, 21*(6), 242–248. doi: 10.5811/WestJet.2020.7.46958

Daldanise, G. (2020). From place-branding to community-branding: A collaborative decision-making process for cultural heritage enhancement. *Sustainability* (Basel, Switzerland), *12*(24), 10399.

Delfini, F., Jr. (2014). Shaping incentives toward effective collaboration: Lessons for conservation practice. *Public Administration Review, 74*(2), 231–232. doi: 10.1111/puar.12201

Downs, A. (1967). *Inside bureaucracy*. Boston, MA: Little, Brown & Company.

Drislane, L. E., & Patrick, C. J. (2017). Integrating alternative conceptions of psychopathic personality: A latent variable model of triarchic psychopathy constructs. *Journal of Personality Disorders, 31*(1), 110–132.

Dubovsky, S., Gorbenko, V., & Mirbabayi, M. (2013). Natural tuning: Towards a proof of concept. *The Journal of High Energy Physics, 2013*(9), 1–24.

Elder, L., & Paul, R. (2004). Becoming a critic of your thinking. Retrieved January 26, 2013 from Foundation for Critical Thinking website: http://www.criticalthinking.org/pages/becoming-a-critic-of-your-thinking/478

Elster, J. (2008). *Reason and rationality*. Princeton: Princeton University Press.

Feiock, R., Lee, I., &Park, H. (2012). Administrators' and elected officials' collaboration networks: Selecting partners to reduce risk in economic development. *Public Administration Review*, *72*(s1), S58–S68. doi: 10.lll/j.1540-6210.2012.02659.x

Final Child & Family Services Review Report (2015). https://1lbxcx1bcuig1rf xaq3rd6w9-wpengine.netdna-ssl.com/wp-content/uploads/2016/06/NC_CFSR _Final_Report.pdf

Fitzgerald, J., & Wolak, J. (2014). The roots of trust in local government in western Europe. *International Political Science Review*, *37*, 130–146. doi: 10.1177%2F0192512114545119

Franklin, C. (2013). Developing expertise in management decision-making. *Academy of Strategic Management Journal*, *12*(1), 21–37.

Frederickson, H., & Smith, K., (2003). *The public administration theory primer*. Boulder, CO: Westview Press. .

Gandel, S. (2010, October 17). How Blockbuster failed at failing. *Time*. Retrieved from http://www.time.com/time/magazine/article/0,9171,2022624,00.html #ixzz1qYh0pVYW

Gigerenzer, G. (2013). *What is certain logic? TEDx December 9, 2013*. Max Plank Institute lecture series. https://www.youtube.com/watch?v=g4op2WNc1e4

Gil, N., Pinto, J. K., & Msulwa, R. S. (2018). Collective strategizing: The UK Government's polycentric approach to plan HS2. *Academy of Management Proceedings*, *2018*(1), 17726. doi: 10.5465/AMBPP.2018.17726abstract

Gjersten, A. (2014). Legitimacy in interlocal partnerships: Balancing efficiency and democracy. *Urban Studies (Edinburgh, Scotland)*, *51*(9), 1926–1942. doi: 10.1177/0042098013502828

Górecki, T., & Smaga, Ł. (2015). A comparison of tests for the one-way ANOVA problem for functional data. *Computational Statistics*, *30*(4), 987–1010.

Gounaris, S., & Koritos, C. D. (2012). Adoption of technologically based innovations: The neglected role of bounded rationality. *The Journal of Product Innovation Management*, *29*(5), 821–838.

Greenwood, N., Ellmers, T., & Holley, J. (2014). The influence of ethnic group composition on focus group discussions. *BMC Medical Research Methodology*, *14*, 107. doi: 10.1186/1471-2288-14-107

Grimmelikhuijsen, S., Jilke, S., Olsen, A. L., & Tummers, L. (2017). Behavioral public administration: Combining insights from public administration and psychology. *Public Administration Review*, *77*, 45–56. doi: 10.1111/puar.12609

Gsottbauer, E., & van den Bergh, J. C. J. M. (2011). Environmental policy theory given bounded rationality and other-regarding preferences. *Environmental & Resource Economics*, *49*(2), 263–304.

Guest, G., MacQueen, K., M., & Namey, E. E. (2014). *Applied thematic analysis*. Thousand Oaks, CA: Sage.

Hammond, J. S., Keeny, R. L., & Raiffa, H. (2006, January). The hidden traps in decision making. *Harvard Business Review*. 84(1), 3–9.

Harris, J. (2007). Good leadership: A company's #1 asset. *Business Credit, 109*(9), 12.

Hartley, J., Alford, J., Hughes, O., & Yates, S. (2015). Public value and political astuteness in the work of public managers: The art of the possible. *Public Administration, 93*(1), 195–211. doi: 10.1111/padm.12125

HB 630/Session Law 2017-41: Rylan's Law. https://files.nc.gov/ncosbm/documents/files/ChildWelfareReform_FinalPlan.pdf

Humphries, A. S., & Wilding, R. D. (2004). Long-term collaborative business relationships: The impact of trust and C3 behaviour. *Journal of Marketing Management, 20*, 1107–1122. doi: 10.1362/0267257042405240

Hunt, S. T. (2014). *Common sense talent management: Using strategic human resources to improve company performance*. San Francisco, CA: Jossey-Bass.

Hyman, D. A., & Kovacic, W. E. (2020). State enforcement in a polycentric world. *Brigham Young University Law Review, 2019*(6), 1447–1470, 1447A.

Ibrahim, M., & Khaimah, R. A. (2009). Theory of bounded rationality. *Public Management, 91*(5), 3.

Isett, K. R., Mergel, I. A., LeRoux, K., Mischen, P. A., & Rethemeyer, R. K. (2011). Networks in public administration scholarship: Understanding where we are and where we need to go. *Journal of Public Administration Research & Theory, 21*(1), 157–173. doi: 10.1093/jopart/muq061

Jarvie, D. (2018). Do long-time team-mates lead to better team performance? A social network analysis of data from major league baseball. *Sports Medicine (Auckland), 48*(11), 2659–2669. doi: 10.1007/s40279-018-0970-9

Jordan, S., Brimbal, L., Wallace, D. B., Kassin, S. M., Hartwig, M., & Street, C. N. H. (2019). A test of the micro expressions training tool: Does it improve lie detection? *Journal of Investigative Psychology & Offender Profiling, 16*(3), 222–235. doi: 10.1002/jip.1532

Jorgensen, T. B., & Rutgers, M. R. (2015). Public values: Core or confusion? Introduction to the centrality and puzzlement of public values research. *American Review of Public Administration, 45*, 3–18. doi: 10.1177/0275074014545781

Khalil, M. H., Shebl, M. K., Kosba, M. A., El-Sabrout, K., & Zaki, N. (2016). Estimate the contribution of incubation parameters influence egg hatchability using multiple linear regression analysis. *Veterinary World, 9*(8), 806–810.

Kim, S. (2017;2019;). The process model of corporate social responsibility (CSR) communication: CSR communication and its relationship with consumers' CSR knowledge, trust, and corporate reputation perception. *Journal of Business Ethics, 154*(4), 1143–1159. doi: 10.1007/s10551-017-3433-6

Kim, Y. & Darnall, N. (2015). Business as a collaborative partner: Understanding firms' sociopolitical support for policy formation. *Public Administration Review, 76*(2), 326–337. doi: 10.1111/puar.12463

Koumakhov, R. (2009). Conventions in herbert Simon's theory of bounded rationality. *Journal of Economic Psychology, 30*(3), 293–306.

Krames, J. A. (2003). *What the best CEOs know: 7 Exceptional leaders and their lessons for transforming any business*. New York: McGraw-Hill.

Krebsbach, M. R. T. (2017). The totality of the circumstances: The DoD law of war manual and the evolving notion of direct participation in hostilities. *Journal of National Security Law & Policy, 9*(1), 125–157.

Krnc, M., & Škrekovski, R. (2020). Group degree centrality and centralization in networks. *Mathematics (Basel), 8*(1810), 1810. doi: 10.3390/math8101810

Langdon, J. L. (2020). Examining the connections between the work we do and our mental health: National Association for kinesiology in higher education 29th delphine hanna commemorative lecture 2020. *Quest (00336297), 72*(2), 119–133. doi: 10.1080/00336297.2020.1736107

LeRoux, K., Brandenburger, P. W., & Pandey, S. K. (2010). Interlocal service cooperation in US cities: A social network explanation. *Public Administration Review, 70*(2), 268–278, 190–191.

LiCalzi, M., & Surucu, O. (2012). The power of diversity over large solution spaces. *Management Science, 58*(7), 1408–1421.

Mador, M. (2000.) Strategic decision making process research: Are entrepreneur and owner managed firms different? *Journal of Research in Marketing and Entrepreneurship, 2*(3), 215–234. doi: 10.1108/14715200080001547

Marino, K., Wright, R. (2015). Decision making in child protective services investigations: why do cases languish in the system? White paper for NC DHHS.

Martinsuo, M., & Hoverfält, P. (2018). Change program management: Toward a capability for managing value-oriented, integrated multi-project change in its context. *International Journal of Project Management, 36*(1), 134–146. doi: 10.1016/j.ijproman.2017.04.018

McCullough, J. M. (2017). Local health and social services expenditures: An empirical typology of local government spending. *Preventive Medicine, 105*, 66–72. doi: 10.1016/j.ypmed.2017.08.018

McCurdy, H. E. (1991). Organizational decline: NASA and the life cycle of bureaus. *Public Administration Review, 4*, 308.

Meier, K. J., & O'Toole, L. J. (2003). Public management and educational performance: The impact of managerial networking. *Public Administration Review, 63*(6), 689–699.

Melander, L., & Lakemond, N. (2015). Governance of supplier collaboration in technologically uncertain NPD projects. *Industrial Marketing Management, 49*, 116–127. doi: 10.1016/j.indmarman.2015.04.006

Mellahi, K., & Collings, D. G. (2010). The barriers to effective global talent management: The example of corporate élites in MNEs. *Journal of World Business, 45*(2), 143–149.

Mintzberg, H. (1987, July/August). Crafting strategy. *Harvard Business Review.* 71, 66–75.

Molinengo, G., & Stasiak, D. (2020). Scripting, situating, and supervising: The role of artifacts in collaborative practices. *Sustainability, 12*(16), 6407. doi:10.3390/su12166407

Monahan, E. L., Hoffman, B. J., Lance, C. E., Jackson, D. J. R., & Foster, M. R. (2013). Now you see them, now you do not: The influence of indicator-factor ratio on support for assessment center dimensions. *Personnel Psychology, 66*(4), 1009–1047

Multiple Response System (MRS) Evaluation Report (2009).

Murray, C. H. (2002). *Executive decision making* (6th ed.). Newport, RI: U.S. Naval War College.

NC Child Protective Services Evaluation (2016) https://files.nc.gov/ncdhhs/documents/files/dss/statistics/NC-Statewide-CPS-Evaluation-02-26-16.pdf

Olsen, B. J., Parayitam, S., & Bao, B. (2007). Strategic decision making: The effects of cognitive diversity, conflict, and trust on decision outcomes. *Journal of Management, 33*, 196–222. doi: 10.1177%2F0149206306298657

Osborne, S.P. (Ed.). (2010). *The new public governance?: Emerging perspectives on the theory and practice of public governance* (1st ed.). Routledge.

Pascarella, P. (1997). The secret of turning thinking into action. *Management Review, 86*(5), 38–39.

Paul, R. W. (1990). *Critical thinking: What every person needs to survive in a rapidly changing world.* Rohner Park, CA: Sonoma State University Press.

Philley, J. (2005). Critical thinking concepts. *Professional Safety, 50*(3), 26–32.

Porter, B. E. (2011). Serving two masters. *Mechanical Engineering, 133*(8), 30–34.

Potapchuk, W. (2016). Goals and collaborative advantage: What's the relationship? *Public Administration Review,* 76(6), 925–927. doi: 10.1111/puar.12678

Power, D. J. (2007). *A brief history of decision support systems.* Retrieved March 10, 2014, from http://DSSResources.COM/history/dsshistory.html

Rainey, H. (Ed.), Bryson, J., & Ackermann, F. (2016). Discovering collaborative advantage: The contributions of goal categories and visual strategy mapping. *Public Administration \Review,* 76(6), 9 12–925. doi: 10.1111/puar.12608

Richardson, K. A. (2008). Managing complex organizations: Complexity thinking and the science and art of management. *Emergence: Complexity & Organization, 10*(2), 13–26.

Rochefort, D. A. (2019). Innovation and its discontents: Pathways and barriers in the diffusion of assertive community treatment. *The Milbank Quarterly.* doi: 10.1111/1468-0009.12429

Rossi, P. H., Lipsey, M. W., & Freeman, H. E. (2004). *Evaluation: a systematic approach* (2nd ed.). Sage Publications.

Rutgers, M. R. (2015). As good as it gets? On the meaning of public value in the study of policy and management. *The American Review of Public Administration, 45*, 29–45. doi: 10.1177/0275074014525833

Salehi, A., Harris, N., Marzban, M., & Coyne, E. (2015). Confirmatory factor analysis of scales measuring trust, and control-self-efficacy of young iranian women. *Social Indicators Research, 124*(3), 1033–1047.

Sanders, R. (1999). *The executive decision-making process: Identifying problems and assessing outcomes.* Westport, CT: Quorum.

Schoenburg, B. (2008). *Critical thinking in business.* Chesterfield, MO: Heuristic Books.

Scriven, M., & Paul, R. (1987). *The critical thinking community.* Retrieved May 6, 2013 from http://www.criticalthinking.org/pages/defining-critical-thinking/766

Semanchin Jones, A. (2015). Implementation of differential response: A racial equity analysis. *Child Abuse & Neglect, 39*, 73–85. doi: 10.1016/j.chiabu.2014.04.013

Shadid, W. K. (2018). A framework for managing organizations in complex environments. *Construction Management & Economics, 36*(4), 182–202. doi: 10.1080/01446193.2017.1343483

Shapiro, S. (2010). Decision-making under pressure. *Futurist, 44*(1), 42–44.

Shrestha, M. (2017). Network structure, strength of relationships, and communities' success in project implementation. *Public Administration Review, 78*(2), pp. 284–294. doi: 10.1111/puar.12787

Shutters, S. T., Lobo, J., Muneepeerakul, R., Strumsky, D., Mellander, C., Brachert, M., & Bettencourt, L. M. A. (2018). Urban occupational structures as information networks: The effect on network density of increasing number of occupations. *PloS One, 13*(5), doi: 10.1371/journal.pone.0196915

Siddiki, S., Kim, J., & William, L. (2017). Diversity, trust, and social learning in collaborativegovernance. *Public Administration Review, 77*(6), 863–874. doi: 10.1111/puar.12800

Simon, H. A. (1947). *Administrative behavior: A study of decision-making processes in administrative organization.* New York: Macmillan.

Simon, H. A. (1949). *Administrative behavior: A study in the decision-making process in administrative organization.* New York: Macmillan.

Simon H.. A. (1962). The architecture of complexity. *Proceedings of the American Philosophical Society, 106*(6), 467–482. doi: https://www.jstor.org/stable/985254

Simon, H. A. (1983). *Reason in human affairs.* Stanford, CA: Stanford University Press.

Simon H. A. (1991) Bounded rationality and organizational learning. *Organization Science, 2*(1), 125–134. doi: 10.1287/orsc.2.1.125

Simon, H. A. (1996). *Models of my life.* Boston, MA: MIT Press.

Simon, H. A. (1996), *The sciences of the artificial* (3rd ed.). The MIT Press.

Simon, H. A. (1997). *Administrative behavior: A study in the decision-making process in administrative organization* (4th ed.). New York: Macmillan.

Simon, H. A. (2000). *John Gaus Lecture,* Paper presented at the annual meeting of the American Political Science Association, Chicago, IL.

Simon, H. A. (2000). John Gaus Lecture. Personal Collection of Herber A. Simon, Carnegie Mellon University, Pittsburgh, PA.

Simon, H. A. (2002). Near decomposability and the speed of evolution. *Industrial and Corporate Change, 11*(3), 587–599. doi: 10.1093/icc/11.3.587

Sloan, D. V. (2017). Total quality management in the culture of higher education. *The Review of Higher Education, 17*(4), 447–464. doi: 10.1353/rhe.1994.0012

Song, M., Park, J., & Kyujin, J. (2017). *Do political similarities facilitate interlocal collaboration? Public Administration Review, 78*(2), 261–269.

Speak, B., & Muncer, S. (2014;2015;). The structure and reliability of the health of the nation outcome scales. *Australasian Psychiatry: Bulletin of the Royal Australian and New Zealand College of Psychiatrists, 23*(1), 66–68.

Stewart, W. P., Liebert, D., & Larkin, K. W. (2004). Community identities as visions for landscape change. *Landscape and Urban Planning, 69,* 315–334. doi: 10.1016/j.landurbplan.2003.07.005

Sullivan, R. P. (2020). Revitalizing fourth amendment protections: A true totality of the circumstances test in § 1983 probable cause determinations. *Iowa Law Review*, *105*(2), 687–734.

Sun, R. & Henderson, A. (2016). Transformational leadership and organizational processes: Influencing public performance. *Public Administration Review*, 77(4), 554–565. doi: 10.1111/puar.1265

Termeer, C. J. A. M., & Dewulf, A. (2019). A small wins framework to overcome the evaluation paradox of governing wicked problems. *Policy and Society*, *38*(2), 298–314. doi: 10.1080/14494035.2018.1497933

Thomson, A., Nayak, P., Plunkett, M., & Kallappa, C. (2014). G170(P) Child protection and safeguarding training - is simulation training effective? *Archives of Disease in Childhood*, 99 (Supl. 1) A75.

Välilä, T. (2020). An overview of economic theory and evidence of public-private partnerships in the procurement of (transport) infrastructure. *Utilities Policy, 62*, 100995. doi: 10.1016/j.jup.2019.100995

Van Stigt, R., Driessen, P. P. J., & Spit, T. J. M. (2015). A user perspective on the gap between science and decision-making: Local administrators' views on expert knowledge in urban planning. *Environmental Sciences & Policy, 47*, 167–176. doi: 10.1016/j.envsci.2014.12.002

Wang, J., Zhang, Z., & Jia, M. (2019). Echoes of corporate social responsibility: How and when does CSR influence employees' promotive and prohibitive voices? JBE. *Journal of Business Ethics, 1*–17. doi:10.1007/s10551-019-04151-6

Wang, Y., Liu, J., Gao, R., & Hwang, B. (2020). government subsidies in public-private partnership projects based on altruistic theory. *International Journal of Strategic Property Management, 24*(3), 153–164. doi:10.3846/ijspm.2020.11545

Waugh Jr., W. & Streib, G. (2006). Collaboration and leadership for effective emergency management. *Public Administration Review, 66*(s1), 131–140. doi: 10.1111/j.1540-6210.2006.00673.x

Weber, E. (2009). Explaining institutional change in tough cases of collaboration: "Ideas" in the blackfoot watershed. *Public Administration Review, 69*(2), 314–327.

Welch, D. A. (2001). *Decisions, decisions: The art of effective decision-making*. Amherst, NY: Prometheus Books.

Westbrook, T., & Marino, K. (2019). Simulation training innovations in childl protective services: A North Carolina Western Region proof of concept. Technical Research for the NCACDSS.

Westbrook, T., Ellett, A., & Asberg, K. (2012). Predicting public child welfare employees' intentions to remain employed with the child welfare organizational culture inventory. *Children and Youth Services Review, 34*, 1214–1221.

Wiebe, S. M. (2015). Decolonizing engagement? creating a sense of community through collaborative filmmaking. *Studies in Social Justice*, 9(2), 244–257.

Wilson, M. (2004). *Constructing measures: An item response modeling approach*. Mahwah, NJ: Lawrence Erlbaum Associates.

Wright, R. & Marino, K. (2019, September). *Administrative tethering: An examination of key findings of a state level collaboration within North Carolina's child protective services*. Paper presented at the annual meeting of the National Center for Public Performance, Boston, MA.

Wolgast, K. A. (2005). *Command decision-making: Experience counts*. Carlisle, PA: U.S. Army War College.

Wright, R. & Marino, K. (2020, September). *Toward a theoretical construct of administrative tethering*. Paper presented at the annual meeting of the Northeast Conference of Public Administration, Boston, MA.

Wright, R. & Shiner, J. (2017). Managing collaboration in e-procurement in D*igital Governance and E-Government Principles Applied to Public Procurement*, 2017. doi: 10.4018/978-1-5225-2203-4.ch004

Wright, R. (2009). Key performance measure considerations in implementation & policy design: Assessing the workforce investment act program. *International Journal of Knowledge, Culture and Change Management, 9*(7), 89–110.

Wulf, A., & Butel, L. (2017). Knowledge sharing and collaborative relationships in business ecosystems and networks. *Industrial Management and Data Systems, 117*, 1407–1425. doi: 10.1108/IMDS-09-2016-0408

Yi, H. (2017). Network structure and governance performance: What makes a difference? *Public Administration Review, 78*(2), 195–205. doi: 10.1111/puar.12886

Yin, R. k. (2014). *Case study research: Design and methods* (5th ed.). Thousand Oaks, CA: Sage.

Zakharina, O., Khodakivskii, E., Iakobchuk, V., & Zhytomyr National Agroecological University. (2020). Explication of the concept of «public-private partnership» in public administration theory. *Scientific Horizons, 88*(3), 26–33. doi: 10.33249/2663-2144-2020-88-3-26-33

Zavalloni, M., Raggi, M., & Viaggi, D. (2019). Agri-environmental policies and public goods: An assessment of coalition incentives and minimum participation rules. *Environmental Resource Economics, 72*, 1023–1040. doi: 10.1007/s10640-018-0237-9

Zhang, F. & Feeney, M. (2017). Managerial ambivalence and electronic civic engagement: The role of public manager beliefs and perceived needs. *Public Administration Review, 78*(1), 5870. doi: 10.1111/puar.12853

Zhang, L., Seale, H., Wu, S., Yang, P., Zheng, Y., Ma, C., . . . Wang, Q. (2014). Post-pandemic assessment of public knowledge, behavior, and skill on influenza prevention among the general population of beijing, china. *International Journal of Infectious Diseases, 24*, 1–5.

Zhao, L., Wang, R., Liu, S., & Yan, J. (2017). Validation of chinese version of the 4-item trust in nurses scale in patients with cancer. *Patient Preference and Adherence, 11*, 1891–1896.

Zori, S., & Morrison, B. (2009). Critical thinking in nurse managers. *Nursing Economics, 27*(2), 75–79.

Index

About the Authors

Dr. Kevin Marino grew up in the mountains of western North Carolina. He has served children and families throughout his adulthood in various roles from youth pastor to executive leadership in social service organizations. An advocate for both frontline social workers and families, his calling in education, training, and collaboration continues to shape healthier futures for those served in his home state.

Dr. Robert James Wright hails from north of Boston, Massachusetts in Salem, Massachusetts. He spent his childhood in the small town of Middleton, MA, and his formative years in Chicago, IL. He has developed his interest in collaboration, over the last several decades, serving both as a practitioner and academician. He holds a BA from the University of Chicago, an MPA from Suffolk University, Boston, MA, and a Doctorate in Public Administration from the University of LaVerne, LaVerne, CA. He enjoys tending to his tomato plants and feeding the birds, armed with the keen insights and guidance provided by his dear wife, Mary.